EDWARD THE SECOND

SUDDENLY, AT BERKELEY

R. PERRY
1988

Photographs by Marc Giddings
Except where otherwise acknowledged

Cover Design, Drawings and Maps
by Victor Jellings

© R. Perry 1988
Reprint 1996, 2007

ISBN 0 95140280 3

Published by Ivy House Books, 30 Porthill Road,
Shrewsbury SY3 8SA

Printed by Manor Printing Services (Wotton) Ltd.,
The Abbey Business Park,
Kingswood, Wotton-under-Edge, Gloucestershire

EDWARD THE SECOND

SUDDENLY, AT BERKELEY

CONTENTS

ILLUSTRATIONS

Maps

FOREWORD

by

MR JOHN BERKELEY

Dr. Perry has brought alive vividly in this book the intrigue, the brutality, the splendour of feudal England in the Fourteenth Century. Those were the days when brawn counted for more than brain, when skill in the martial arts counted for more than eloquent learning, when only the strongest and most devious survived.

King Edward II, weak in moral fibre and the pawn of unworthy companions, contrasted starkly with his father and his son, both of whom knew how to contend with their rebellious subjects. The king's pitiful death here at Berkeley Castle closed the life of a man who sadly squandered his talents.

In this book Dr. Perry has illustrated most ably the characters of those who surrounded the king and those who opposed him. My family were in the thick of events at that time, some members coming out of those events with credit, others not so well. However the reader may judge them, it is certain that the author has carried out tireless research into events that happened more than six centuries ago.

Although some of those events must be conjecture in the absence of documentary proof, nevertheless historically this book is as accurate in its facts as it can possibly be. I find it fascinating, and I recommend it to all who, like me, find the story of Edward II compulsive reading.

R. J. Berkeley
Berkeley Castle

CHAPTER ONE

AS THE TWIGS WERE BENT

'Tis Education forms the common mind,
Just as the twig is bent, the tree's inclin'd.
ALEXANDER POPE.

On the May morning when Thomas, Lord Berkeley rode out of his castle at the head of a formidable band of fighting men, the delicate green of the elm tree leaves and the white hawthorn blossom were proclaiming that spring had come to the Vale of Severn. So began, in the year 1300, a long unhurried march to Carlisle.

An upstart Scottish knight, William Wallace, had seized some English-held castles across the border and that formidable old worrior, Edward I, had summoned his barons to come in person, bringing their due contingents of men for a campaign that would subdue, once and for all, these northern rebels.

Thomas had received such a call many times. He had contracted to serve his king with his eldest son, eight knights and thirteen mounted men-at-arms, not just for the annual forty days owed by all barons, but for every campaign, however long. For this he and his men were on the royal pay-roll: four shillings a day for himself as an experienced commander, two shillings for each knight or man-at-arms, a shilling for each squire.

In all, the Berkeley company numbered some two hundred men. In medieval warfare the role of the heavily armed knight and his armoured horse was, like that of the modern tank, to break into and disorganise the ranks of the enemy. Like the tank, the knight needed infantrymen to follow him into battle to complete the rout.

For this expedition he had also been commissioned to recruit two hundred longbowmen from the Forest of Dean at sixpence a day and a team

1

of miners whose job it was to tunnel under the walls of any castle that would not surrender. It would be a long hard slog for these footmen. Some of them would march a thousand miles before they saw Gloucestershire again. Did they ever manage to hitch a lift? Did anyone ever ride home on a "liberated" Scottish pony? However they travelled they must have been a hardy set of men. There was never any difficulty about recruitment. The pay was not only good, it was in actual money, which they did not often see. And for young men the summer campaign brought relief from the boredom of winter and the tedium of family life. There was the prospect of excitement, of violence and, above all, opportunities for plunder.

With the company travelled a train of packhorses and wagons loaded with tents for the notables, armour and weapons, corn and portable mills for grinding it. Grooms led the great destriers, the stallion war-horses, ancestors of the modern Shire, that were ridden only in tournament and battle. There were the mounted falconers with their peregrines and goshawks, huntsmen with coursing dogs and twenty couple of deerhounds, servants and attendants of all kinds.

As the Berkeley contingent moved northwards from Gloucester through Hereford and Shropshire they renewed friendships with the Marcher Lords alongside whom they had always fought. The de Clares of Gloucester, the Bohuns of Hereford, Mortimers of Wigmore and Ludlow were all preparing to join their king at Carlisle. Though they would not all follow the same route at the same time, there were many occasions when old companions could gather. Sometimes there was a stay of a few days in one of the Mortimer castles for the hunting and hawking to be had in the border lands of Wales.

Enjoyable though these summer journeys could be for the participants the almost annual passage of ill-disciplined archers and hangers-on was not welcomed by people of the towns and villages through which they passed. Barons and their immediate retainers could be expected to pay for what they needed but cattle and sheep wandering on common land fell an easy prey to hungry footmen. Precious stores of grain were apt to disappear without hope of payment. It was prudent, too, to keep wives and daughters safely indoors until the soldiery had passed.

By Midsummer Day all had reached Carlisle: a great company of knights and troopers, archers, spearmen and engineers and lawless rabble of camp followers. This army marched into Scotland in four columns or "battles", colourful with scores of banners, surcoats and innumerable pennants.

The fourth column was under the nominal command of the seventeen year old Edward of Carnarvon, the future Edward II. Before him was carried the royal standard, distinguished by the azure label of an elder son. His father had decided that the time had come to apprentice him to the grim business of war. No medieval king could hope to dominate the stern territorial magnates unless he was seen to be a fearless leader in battle and, what was even more important, a successful organiser of campaigns, for the making of profitable war was an essential skill of kingship. The earlier a prince was blooded the less likely was he to meet with trouble after his accession.

Around the prince his father had placed young knights of proven courage who would serve as exemplars. By his side rode Maurice de Berkeley, eldest son of Thomas, only four years older than the prince but already a veteran of five campaigns in Wales, Scotland and France. Two years before he had fought in the great pitched battle of Falkirk. Maurice had first looked Mars in the face as a boy of fourteen, serving against the Welsh. He was a precocious young man. In that same year he had fathered a son, a younger Thomas, now seven years old and destined by fate to be the gaoler of the future king.

Maurice was not the only Berkeley in the field. His father had brought two other sons and half a dozen brothers, nephews and cousins. This march into Scotland for the first time brought the Berkeleys into close association with Prince Edward; during the next twenty-seven years their lives became ever more interwoven, until the final tragedy in the castle keep at Berkeley.

The army moved westwards along the shore of the Solway Firth. Roads were crowded with troops of knights led by their bannerets, straggling companies of infantry, baggage teams. On the calm sea a fleet of fifty ships moved on a parallel course. The days were long and spirits high. The Scots watched from the hills, offering no resistance. On the fourth day the leading column crossed the Lochan Water and came to the castle of Caerlaverock, rose red against a background of sea and woodland.

Only a few years earlier it had been built at Edward I's orders to guard the road to Carlisle and England but as a result of some surprise attack or piece of treachery it had fallen into the hands of Wallace. It was not a great stronghold but it was a formidable little fortification. On a shelf of sandstone, protected by marshy land and a moat, it could be attacked only from one side. Triangular in shape, with a tower at each of the base corners

Caerlaverock Castle.

and a strong gatehouse at its northern apex, its defenders could cover every approach. Though its military importance was small the garrison of sixty men at arms, if left in possession, could harass the English lines of communication and give shelter to prowling partisans. Above all, its recovery was a matter of prestige.

For the benefit of the prince's education a set piece siege was mounted: a sledge-hammer to crack a nut. Tents were pitched, servants unpacked tapestries to hang in the royal pavilion and those of the great lords, silver vessels were placed on the trestle tables, floors were strewn with herbs and flowers. Minstrels played and sang whilst their masters drank the red wine of Bordeaux and talked of past exploits and future triumphs. Before Lord Thomas's tent was displayed, according to custom, the heraldic shield of the Berkeleys bearing the silver chevron and ten crosses on a red ground. In contrast to the eve of a great battle, the atmosphere was light-hearted.

Next morning the heralds went forward to demand surrender. The Scots were defiant, refusing to be overawed by the huge army now surrounding them, so the siege began. Footmen advance to the edge of the outer moat aiming their arrows and the iron quarrels of crossbows at the defenders on the walls who replied with more arrows and showers of stones. The English had the worst of these exchanges, standing as they did exposed to fire, protected only by leather jerkins. Many were killed or wounded before the survivors were withdrawn. This routine opening was followed by an assault of men-at-arms on the drawbridge and gatehouse but they too were driven back.

It was now the turn of the younger barons and the knights. The herald whose chronicle is the source of our information, tells us that

'They did not advance like cautious men
Nor as persons skilled in such affairs,
But as men influenced and blinded by pride
Riding forward to the very edge of the moat.'

What they could do here, apart from the ritual brandishing of lances and shouting of taunts, is not apparent but according to the herald whose job it was to celebrate their courage and skill they performed many feats of valour and young Maurice Berkeley gets a 'mention in despatches' for his bravery. The knights were met with showers of stones; it may well be that the defenders were careful not to use more deadly weapons; the deaths of a dozen young men of noble families might have dire consequences if surrender became necessary.

So the Scots sheltered safely within the walls until the situation was changed by the arrival of a ship carrying the siege train. One Brother Robert, the military engineer in charge, carefully surveyed the ground and began the erection of his war machines. Soon trebuchet and mangon were catapulting balls of stone weighing a hundredweight or more at the gatehouse. Barrels of flaming tar were projected over the walls and arblasts threw javelins into the courtyard. Miners began the tunnels that would undermine the walls and bring them crashing down.

From dawn to dusk Brother Robert's machines discharged missiles that split everything they struck. The destruction became unendurable, food became scarce and casualties mounted. A pennon was put out in token of surrender. The gates were thrown open and those of the garrison who were not dead or wounded filed out. By the custom of the period they thus escaped the slaughter that always followed a successful assault, though one account says that the king hung some traitors he found in the castle. Although barons and knights were given the herald's praise, it was already becoming apparent that technicians of humble birth, like Brother Robert, were more effective than noble exponents of knightly combat.

The capture of Caerlaverock decided nothing. Apart from one brief skirmish when the prince first rode beneath a shower of arrows, all attempts to bring the Scots to battle failed. The fine weather of July gave way to a wet and dismal August; Wallace and his men disappeared into the hills of Galloway, a land of bogs, awkward little rivers and dark forests. The peasants drove their cattle into these fastnesses, parties of English foragers were ambushed and food was hard to come by. As for plunder, there was little to be had and no one worth a ransom to be captured.

The knights grumbled, the infantry began to desert. The king, angry and irritable, led the way back to Carlisle and England. An expensive campaign had produced no results. For the young prince it was an unfortunate introduction to war. The Berkeleys made the long journey back to Gloucestershire, less exuberant now but no doubt philosophic about their disappointment. After all, it was routine work for professional soldiers for which they were well paid, though usually they had to wait some time for their money.

Thomas de Berkeley was one of the king's most trusted and valued barons. He had fought at Edward's side for thirty-five years ever since the king, as Prince Edward, had defeated Simon de Montfort at the battle of Evesham. In his lifetime he took part in nearly thirty campaigns, in one of them holding office as Constable of the whole army, a post usually held by one of the great earls. The Berkeleys were never members of the most powerful group of magnates, the earls who with the king effectively governed the country, but from the first they were summoned to the King's Council and to the Parliaments of Edward I.

Thomas was ranked thirty-seventh in the roll of about a hundred barons. He was lord of a compact group of fertile manors in the Severn Vale which had been given by Henry II to his ancestor Robert Fitzharding, a wealthy Bristol merchant and financier. To these had been added by inheritance, marriage and purchase many others in the southern counties of England.

Young Maurice de Berkeley was born into a household of more than two hundred persons: knights and esquires, valets and pages, troopers and yeomen, grooms and servants. In the stables were a hundred horses and palfreys, ready for the annual call to arms.

Berkeley Castle. South front.

The atmosphere was wholly martial. When not at war the Berkeleys kept in training at tournaments, which had now developed from savage melees reproducing the conditions of the battlefield into carefully regulated series of individual combats. They were now recognised social occasions and great sporting events, the fourteenth century equivalent of Ascot or the Grand National. But those who took part in a "Round Table" ran almost as much risk of death as in actual warfare. Thomas de Berkeley himself had only inherited after the death of his elder brother in a famous tournament at Kenilworth.

Though the danger was considerable, rewards could be substantial. By custom, the armour, weapons and even the mount of the defeated were forfeit to the victor. Since knights often wagered large sums on their chance of success they could return home much richer or, occasionally, almost destitute.

Each combat followed a set pattern. The two knights, in full armour and crested helm, with shields held to protect neck and chest, settled themselves in their saddles and gripped their lances firmly. Spurring their horses they galloped towards each other in the straightest possible line, aiming to strike their opponent's shield or helm a square blow that would unseat him. Such a blow might splinter a lance, split a shield, hurl the horse back on his haunches, unhelm the rider or send him crashing to the ground. If a horse swerved so that the riders passed each other, any blow struck from the side was a foul, punished by confiscation of horse and armour. Every tournament ended with its quota of spear wounds, broken limbs, bleeding heads and noses and not unusually a death or two.

John Smyth, the family historian of the Berkeleys, noted that Thomas had attended tournaments at twenty different places, "for him it was almost a monthly exercise". He was an enthusiast, as though war did not give him enough military activity. Young Maurice too was an addict. From the time of his early marriage he seems to have had an establishment of his own on one of his father's Somerset manors "where he frequented those downs in all martial exercises, running with lances, hastiludes, spearplays and the like". These were informal local joustings, but, says Smyth, no year passed when he did not go to public tournaments at Worcester, Dunstable, Stourport or Blyth.

The Berkeleys were keen huntsmen, maintaining horses, hounds and hawks in great numbers. Maurice and his brothers hunted in the forest of Michaelwood and the parks and woodlands of the Cotswold foothills around Wotton-under-Edge, "spending whole nights out in the fields and woods in pursuit of foxes, wild goats, deer and hares".

All these activities were not allowed to interfere with the careful supervision of the Berkeley inheritance. When at home, Thomas was constantly on the move from one manor house to another, visiting each for some days every year, inspecting his flocks of sheep and seeing that his stewards were looking after their lord's interests.

The Berkeley way of life was designed to breed hardy, brave young men for whom the dangers and discomforts of tournament and battlefield were a normal part of baronial life; young men who would grow up to dominate and lead the often turbulent soldiers of their retinue. In three centuries it did not fail to furnish the Berkeley domain with such men.

It was even more important that the king of England should possess this ability. The bond between the barons and the Crown was a practical one; there was no mystical reverence for the monarchy. They expected the king to observe the feudal code, to decide disputes, to listen to the advice of his earls and barons and to lead them in successful and profitable warfare. If he failed in these respects he could expect trouble from the Berkeleys and their like, as King John had found.

Though he was the son of such a famous warrior the prince revealed to the watchful barons on his first campaign none of the qualities of his father. There was admiration for his splendid appearance. Fair haired, more than six feet tall, built like an athlete, he had the look and bearing of a king. However, old soldiers at Caerlaverock noticed that he showed little interest in the military operations. But he was good company. Some of the old hands shook their heads at his habit of drinking and gambling into the small hours, but many of the young men who drank and diced with him found him much to their liking.

"As the twig is bent, the tree's inclin'd" wrote Alexander Pope. The seeds of Edward's misfortunes are to be found in his childhood. His upbringing had not fitted him for medieval warfare or indeed for most aspects of the life of a fourteenth century king of England. His elder brother's early death was a blow to his father, whom seems to have looked on Edward as a second best, more or less ignoring him for many years. For much of the king's time was spent in warfare or in southern France organising the government and defences of his rich province of Aquitaine.

The death of his Spanish wife, Queen Eleanor, left the old king a lonely and irritable man. The increasing cares of state left him little time for his children. The young prince rarely saw him except at Christmas. Then there was no mother there; his father aroused no affection nor felt any himself.

During these childhood years the usual home of the prince was the manor house of Langley: Childe's Langley as it came to be called because of his residence there and, later, King's Langley. It was an attractive little place on the chalk slopes above a little Hertfordshire river. Queen Eleanor had furnished her home with the plate and jewels, Venetian glass, dishes of Damascus ware, ornaments of amber, jet and coral which she had brought with her from the splendid civilisation that had flowered from contact with the Arab culture of southern Spain. From these surroundings, so different from the grim, bleak atmosphere of a fourteenth century baronial castle, the young Edward must have absorbed the love of beauty that remained with him all his life, a love to which the old king was indifferent.

From Spain the queen also brought gardeners who made lawns and rose beds, shady walks and orchards. Nothing could have been less like the forbidding castles her husband built in Wales and Scotland. Beyond the gardens were meadows and a park with tame deer; beside the islets of the river stood water mills. Behind the manor house were stables full of horses and ponies.

Here at Langley the young Edward became familiar with rural life and pursuits. In summer his servants taught him how to row; in winter he skated with them on the ponds. From the farmhands he learned the crafts of hedging and ditching; the blacksmith taught him his skills. Always happy in the company of grooms and gardeners, he joined with them to tend their horses and dig their plots. No one seems to have cared much how he spent his time, though his formal education was not entirely neglected. His frequent visits to St. Alban's Abbey, six miles away, gave him a lasting love of music and song; he delighted to spend time with the monks.

The chief influence on his youth is said to have been that of Walter Reynolds, a priest who joined the household when the prince was ten years old. Reynolds endeared himself by his skill in amateur theatricals, bringing to Langley a troupe of little players, with trumpets and kettledrums. Later he was blamed for encouraging the prince's drinking and gambling habits and the pursuit of pleasure to the neglect of business. But Reynolds, a man of fairly humble family, aroused much jealousy when he became Bishop of

Worcester and eventually Archbishop of Canterbury. The monks who wrote the chronicles of the reign may have been prejudiced.

These tastes and habits Edward carried into manhood. In another age and station he could have been happy as a country gentleman and farmer; in the fourteenth century such pursuits were looked upon as dishonourable. "Neglecting the companionship of the magnates," wrote a chronicler, "he fraternised with actors and singers, carters and ditchers, oarsmen and sailors and others who practised the mechanical arts".

After the Scottish campaign the king gave his son a title and lands worthy of the heir to his throne. In a magnificent ceremony at a parliament held at Lincoln he was proclaimed Prince of Wales and Earl of Chester, endowed with almost all the royal lands in Wales. After a visit to his principality the prince accompanied his father on another unsuccessful invasion of Scotland. All that Thomas de Berkeley had to show for it was the loss of several of his war horses "in that needy and cold climate". As they were worth up to a hundred pounds apiece, the equivalent of some thousands today, it was an expensive expedition for him.

Other campaigns followed. Yet another abortive raid on Galloway, a long march to the Moray Firth, a whole winter spent in Perth. The Berkeleys were always there. "On every side the English burnt hamlets and towns, granges and granaries, empty and full". In 1304 Stirling Castle was taken and Wallace brought a prisoner to London, where he was executed. For a moment it seemed that Scotland was conquered. It was an illusion; lasting bitterness and hostility had been ensured and soon a new leader, the great Robert Bruce, appeared to lead his people.

The prince showed no aptitude for this warfare. It was becoming clear to the old king that his son was simply not the stuff of which ruthless, single-minded generals are made. The prince's extravagance, his friendship with a flamboyant young Gascon knight, Piers Gaveston, angered the king. Edward was banished from his father's presence and for a time forbidden to come within thirty miles of the court.

These profitless campaigns bred pessimism and apathy in the baronage. Scotland, a poor country when the wars began, had been so often plundered that there was now little booty to be had. The chances of ignominious death at the hands of wild hillmen in some obscure ambush rather than in knightly combat, had so greatly increased that there was a marked lack of enthusiasm in the young men of noble families.

Edward I had always looked to these young men to give him a military élite of high courage. To restore the martial spirit of the baronage he resolved upon a magnificent pageant of chivalry. At Pentecost in 1306 all qualified youths who had not yet been knighted were summoned to Westminster for the knighting of Prince Edward, and of themselves, attending with their armour, weapons and horses. Two hundred and sixty-seven tyros responded to the call, each accompanied by at least three knights of his own or allied families. No Berkeley appears on the roll of aspirants. For them no call was needed; it was customary for them to be knighted on the battlefield while they were still in their teens. But Thomas and his sons escorted the sixteen year old John Maltravers, son of a Dorset landowner already betrothed to a Berkeley girl.

The most lavish preparations were made for the ceremony. The aspirants kept their all-night vigil in the abbey; in the morning the prince was knighted by his father. Prince Edward then conferred the accolade upon his fellow aspirants, all of his own generation. This was to be a bond between the future king and those who would be the magnates of his kingdom, a hope that was not to be fulfilled. There in the abbey on that long day were gathered the dramatis personae of Edward's troubled reign; the men of good will and the traitors, the court favourites and the blunt lords of the March, his gaolers and murderers. All knelt before him and swore loyalty; lords who died in battle, on the block and scaffold, or peacefully in their beds; Hugh Despenser and Piers Gaveston, his favourites, done to death by jealous magnates; William Trussell who played the chief part in his ceremonial deposition; John Maltravers, possibly one of his murderers; above all, young Roger Mortimer, who supplanted him in his queen's affections, dethroned him and ordered his murder. Looking on were many others who played their parts in the tragedy. The day ended with a long-remembered banquet and entertainment; the festivities continued for a week.

When all was over the new knights joined the battle-hardened soldiers, the Berkeleys and their peers, in another invasion of Scotland. The realities of the campaign bore little relation to the Arthurian ideals of chivalrous warfare expressed in the oaths that the knights had taken. The countryside was mercilessly ravaged in a march "so bloody and disastrous to the Scottish nation" that all chance of peaceful co-existence was lost for centuries. "The king carried away captive all such as had the least ability to stir", and yet the booty was worthless in comparison with the cost of the war.

The old king returned to England having failed once more to impose his will on the Scots. It was his last campaign. Piers Gaveston and some of the new knights had left without the king's permission before it ended. This led to another bitter and violent quarrel between Edward and his son; Gaveston was banished from the kingdom and went into exile in France. But in the following summer the king died at Lanercost Priory, just south of the border, as he was preparing another invasion. The Berkeleys did not form part of the escort that took his body to Westminster. Almost the last act of the king had been to send Thomas and Maurice on an embassy to Pope Clement V, from which they did not return until the autumn. That he chose them for this mission manifests his trust in them and his opinion of their abilities.

CHAPTER TWO

THE ROAD TO BANNOCKBURN

'The English will never love or honour their
sovereign unless he be victorious and a lover of arms.
JEAN FROISSART: CHRONICLES.

No one could have foreseen that the new reign was to be one of military disaster and baronial rebellion ending in the dethronement and murder of the king. Quarrels between kings and their eldest sons have never been uncommon, but Edward II's disagreements with his father were trivial compared to the open rebellion of the heirs of William the Conqueror and Henry II. Though his barons were sometimes restive and occasionally defiant, the old king's military successes had earned their respect and a long reign of firm government seemed to have given an enviable stability to the monarchy. Though as Prince of Wales Edward II had earned a reputation as an easy-going bon viveur with some very un-baronial tastes in recreation and a lack of proper enthusiasm for war and the tournament, the responsibilities of kingship would surely bring the desirable and necessary changes in the life-style of this stalwart, handsome young man.

However, in September, soon after his father's funeral Edward began badly by leading a brief, half-hearted march into Scotland. Nothing was achieved. Bruce again withdrew into the hills, content to play a waiting game now that his old enemy was dead. Edward, equally glad to be free of the old king's control, returned to London and the pleasures of court life.

Piers Gaveston had been at once recalled from exile, created Earl of Cornwall and loaded with gifts and offices. Edward's infatuation with Piers became obvious to all during the autumn; it was said openly that they were homosexual partners. But what really irked the magnates was his position

14

as the king's adviser in matters of state, to the exclusion of those who had a hereditary right to membership of the Council.

Piers's friendship with the king and the great fortune he now possessed seem to have turned his head. Never exactly self-effacing, his bearing became more affected, his manners more exquisite. The troubles of the reign began with a glittering tournament he staged in December at his newly acquired castle of Wallingford. During those months of exile he had taken part in jousts in France, Burgundy and Flanders, adding to his already considerable skill, in much the same way that an English golfer today sharpens his game on the American circuit.

Now he used his wealth to present a spectacle as magnificent as any he had seen at the court of France. He and his spirited Gascon friends successfully challenged all comers. In the presence of the king, the earls of Arundel, Hereford and Surrey were among the defeated, and even those vastly experienced jousters, Thomas and Maurice de Berkeley, just returned from their embassy, could do no more than hold their own. Chagrined by their discomfiture and angered by Gascon swagger, the earls departed, their dislike of Gaveston turning to hatred.

After the usual Christmas festivities in which, of course, Piers played the most prominent part, Edward crossed the Channel to marry Isabel, the twelve year old daughter of Philip the Fair, most avaricious and ruthless of the kings of France. Thomas and Maurice de Berkeley were with the select group of barons who went with Edward to Boulogne; Piers remained in England as Keeper of the Realm, an office that should have gone to the senior earl. Four kings, of France, Navarre, Sicily and Germany, were present at the wedding with retinues drawn from the noblest families of western Europe. No ill humour or quarrel marred the gathering. There was endless feasting, jousting and hunting, no doubt much to the taste of the Berkeleys, before the return to England.

The coronation of the king and queen followed at once. Isabel's uncles, Charles, Count of Valois and Louis, Count of Evreux came with her, accompanied by many of the proudest nobles of France. Dover and London had never seen such resplendent processions. The coronation was a more brilliant ceremony than any that had gone before. The abbey was flooded with the colour beloved by medieval man. Walter Reynolds's theatrical flair combined with Gaveston's love of display and fine clothes to impress even the blasé courtiers of France.

Bishops and abbots in copes embroidered with gold and silver thread

Edward II. Electrotype of his effigy on the tomb in Gloucester
Cathedral.   National Portrait Gallery. (439)

behind crosses glittering with jewels, flanked by chaplains and attendant clergy, moved with dignity to their appointed places. Thomas de Berkeley had seen the coronation of Edward I, a less splendid occasion. Then he was only a knight in his father's suite; now in furred scarlet gown and coronet he walked in procession with his bodyguard of Maurice and the Berkeley knights, in their red liveries. The Lord Mayor of London, the representatives of the Cinque Ports, followed. Last came the king, surrounded by the great officers of state, to be presented to the people and accepted by acclamation.

The coronation oath was administered. Edward promised to cause law and justice to be executed in all his judgments and to observe laws made by the commonalty of the realm. "All this I promise to do". Later in his reign the magnates were to remind him that this was an oath to be kept.

Then came the celebration of the Mass and the anointing; the fair haired king, standing under a golden canopy, clad in a simple robe of white linen, was touched with consecrated oil. Roger Mortimer of Wigmore, the man destined to deprive him of wife, throne and, finally, life itself, brought the priestly garments, alb, tunicle and girdle of cloth of gold. Piers Gaveston, "so decked in royal purple sewn with pearls that he seemed more like Mars than an ordinary mortal", fastened the golden spurs and presented the Sword of St. Edward. "With this sword do justice, stop the growth of iniquity, protect the Church of God". Finally, Piers stepped forward to present the crown of St. Edward, which was blessed and placed on the king's head before his emthronement.

Then came the long procession of earls and barons, in turn kneeling before the king, placing their hands in his and swearing fealty. "I, Roger Mortimer. . . I, Thomas de Berkeley. . . do become your liege lord of life and limb, of earthly worship, and faith and troth I will bear unto you, to live and die against all manner of folk, so help me God".

At the coronation banquet and the celebrations that followed, Piers was constantly at the king's side. Edward paid so little attention to the bride that her uncles went back to France declaring that he cared more for Gaveston than for his wife, a conclusion also reached by the English magnates. They resented the publicity given to Piers in the abbey ceremonies and the goodwill they had shown to Edward in the first months of his reign continued to fade.

As the hostility to Piers increased it was coupled with criticism of a king who never put on armour to exercise in the tilting yard, when every knight knew that this was the only way to prepare oneself for battle; a king who took no pleasure in the company of solid English barons, preferring to spend his time with a pack of frivolous Gascons. What, for example, was old Thomas de Berkeley, with all those campaigns and half a hundred tournaments behind him, to make of a king who sometimes lay in bed until midday, listening to minstrels?

Even the younger barons felt that the atmosphere of the court was effeminate. Most of them had been brought up in their often remote castles to be landowners, hunters, soldiers. Piers was wholly Gascon; lively, exuberant, fashion conscious, gregarious. He and his friends set the tone; the sober, graceful garments of the last reign gave place to the styles and gay colour of the fourteenth century. A well dressed young man could now appear in bright yellow hose, a scarlet surcoat that hung from his hips like a mini-skirt, a fringed cape in two colours and pointed shoes. Piers presided over all this with ever growing arrogance and ostentation.

All could see that in a few short months the king, under the influence of Piers and of Walter Reynolds, now suddenly elevated to the Chancellorship of England, was deteriorating. Never the most stable of characters, his temper became more uncertain and opposition to his wishes sometimes provoked personal violence. By day he gave himself up to hunting and falconry, in the evening to gambling. As a later chronicler put it, "Piers and Reynolds filled the court with companies of jesters, ruffians, flattering parasites, musicians, and other naughty ribalds, that the king might spend days and nights in jesting, playing, gambling and such other filthie and dishonourable exercises".

The responsibilities of government could not be for long ignored. While Edward frittered his time away, bad news came from the north. One by one the English-held castles in Scotland were being taken; an increasingly confident Bruce was raiding across the border, burning farms and driving away cattle. Parliament had to be called. Thomas de Berkeley received his usual summons and, most unusually, Maurice was called as a baron of Parliament in the lifetime of his father. Perhaps Edward, expecting trouble, was trying to add to the number of barons who might be expected to give him support. But many of the magnates came to Westminster with armed knights and retainers, determined on a show-down. So fiercely insistent were they on the banishment of the hated favourite that Edward lost his nerve and gave in to them. Piers was sent to Ireland as viceroy.

Maurice and a few other barons then led a small task force to the north of

England, where the damage had already been done. Bruce had slipped into Scotland with his booty. It was late in the season; the English lacked numbers and supplies for effective pursuit. Perhaps in the king's absence they also lacked the will.

In the next few years the rift between Edward and the barons grew wider. The Scottish raids continued; the government seemed incapable of dealing with the threat. Typical of Edward's indecision were the writs received by Thomas de Berkeley in 1309. First he was summoned to Newcastle for Michaelmas Day, ready to march against the Scots. Almost immediately this was postponed until All Souls—far too late for an invasion. Before he could set out this was cancelled and he was bidden to a Parliament at York "to consult about measures to be taken"; only for the date to be changed to Westminster in December. "Thus under a weak king wavered the government of the state", observed the chronicler.

By this time Piers had returned from Ireland to resume his old position at court. The barons would have no more of this; in 1310 they succeeded in bringing Edward under control of a committee of twenty-one of their number, the Lords Ordainers, whose approval was necessary for political decisions. When the king tried to ignore this, summoning an army to go against the Scots, only two of the earls and a handful of barons responded. Thomas de Berkeley was ordered to muster and arm all those liable for service in Gloucestershire and to requisition great quantities of wheat, oats and beans. He and Maurice had reached Berwick by September, but all to no purpose. They returned home having achieved nothing.

And so it went on. Next year's campaign was equally ineffective; there is no record of the Berkeleys' service though it is difficult to see how they could have avoided their obligations. All this mustering of armies was expensive. Once again Edward found it necessary to call Parliament to get a grant of money. None was forthcoming until Piers was again exiled. This time he simply went into hiding; many suspected that he was in the king's own apartments. He emerged to join the gay round of Christmas festivities at King's Langley, the much loved manor house that to Edward was a Sandringham. Here with his chosen friends he could by day live again the rural pleasures of his childhood and by night listen to his musicians and singers, watch a play or drink and dice, until baronial menaces faded into dreams of a rose-coloured future of happiness with his beloved Piers.

There was a harsh awakening. In the spring he, Piers and the queen went up to Newcastle, attempting to gather men and supplies for a summer campaign. His cousin Thomas, Earl of Lancaster, the most powerful of the northern magnates and the richest man in England, rose in open rebellion. With four other earls he had sworn an oath to rid the kingdom of Gaveston. When the Scots mounted another raid Edward was caught between them and Lancaster's forces. Somehow he escaped, but the queen, then pregnant with her first child, the future Edward III, was left to shift for herself, narrowly escaping capture. Piers was less fortunate. Seized by the earls, on his way southwards he fell into the hands of the ill-natured Guy, Earl of Warwick, an old enemy who had never forgotten some of the Gascon's wounding insults. Watched by Warwick and two other earls, Piers was brutally beheaded on Blacklow Hill, near Banbury.

Piers's death was a devastating blow to the king, made worse by the realisation that he could do nothing to punish the murderers. His response was to go into seclusion at his Hampshire palace of Clarendon. Here he shut himself off from the world; as though only physical exercise could ease his sorrow he turned again to the rural crafts of his youth, hedging, ditching and felling trees in the company of his farm workers. In these weeks he and his companions dug a ditch that encompassed the whole park. As always, there was criticism of these unkingly activities.

When he returned to London he made yet another attempt to gather an army. Most of the barons had lost all confidence in him. Even that old warrior, Thomas de Berkeley, seems to have had enough. Summoned to bring five hundred footmen from Gloucestershire and the Forest of Dean he sent only a token force, himself staying at home. Edward suspected his loyalty, writing to the sheriff of the county ordering him to join with Thomas, or Sir William Wyllington or Sir William Maunsell, "whichever of them seems most loyal", to raise and arm the rest. Any who refused service were to be arrested. The result of this is not recorded, but Maurice, recently given custody of the castle and city of Gloucester, joined the king for more aimless marches in the north.

After the murder of Gaveston, Edward nursed his hatred of the earls through the long winter, waiting for an opportunity for revenge. This did not come. In the spring of 1313 he gladly left the English political scene to spend Whitsuntide in France. He and the queen were invited to her father's court to take part in festivities that included, among other events, a spectacular piece of pageantry when the three sons of the Duke of Burgundy and many other noble youths were knighted before a great gathering of the magnates of France. Nowhere were these things done so well; Paris was a superb setting. This was much more to Edward's taste than marching through the dreary Scottish lowlands. He prolonged his visit to make a leisurely progress through the pleasant lands of Ponthieu and Montreuil, possessions of the English monarchy where manors were rich and towns prosperous, yielding the king more revenue than Scotland was ever likely to do.

The royal party did not get back to England until mid-July, to find that while they had been enjoying themselves Robert Bruce had as usual been marauding in the northern counties, as well as besieging Stirling so closely that the governor had agreed to surrender the castle if no help reached him before midsummer next year.

The barons were disgusted by Edward's absence when his kingdom was in danger. The time for half-hearted measures was past; they demanded action. The governor of Stirling arrived to plead for help. But when preparations were made early in 1314 there was no very ready response. Even Thomas de Berkeley was unwilling to face another campaign, pleading not unreasonably that at the age of sixty-eight he was entitled to honourable retirement, though Smyth notes that in other ways he was as active as ever. Edward would take no excuses, commanding him "upon his honour and allegiance" to bring his men.

Many others were unenthusiastic. Of the earls, only Gloucester, Pembroke and Hereford were willing to serve in person; the others objected that Parliament had not been called to give approval. Maurice de Berkeley as always stood by his commitment; he and his father began the long march northwards.

The army that eventually took the field may have numbered seven or eight thousand, of whom perhaps seven hundred were knights or mounted troopers, with archers and spearmen from Wales, the Midlands and the north. An enormous baggage and artillery train followed. It seemed that Edward was at last showing energy and determination; English hopes were high. The Scots had probably no more than five thousand spearmen and five hundred light horsemen whose equipment did not compare with that of the English knights.

The story of the great disaster is well known. There were in the English army only a few veterans of Edward I's victories. The young men close to the king had no real battle experience. Most had fought in minor skirmishes, but fifteen years had passed since two large armies came to grips at Falkirk.

The first English attempts at reconnaissance were beaten back in confusion. Wrong decisions were made, the wrong position was taken up; the night before the battle the English spent the night uncomfortably bivouacked on the marsh of Bannockburn below Stirling castle. Next morning the Scots moved to the attack. Gilbert, the young earl of Gloucester, realising that his heavily armed knights could not move quickly on the swampy ground, urged Edward to avoid battle. He was at once accused of cowardice, in the most insulting terms. Stung by the accusation he rode off to join the leading column, only to be involved in another violent quarrel with the earl of Hereford over the right to lead the attack. Gilbert ended this by charging recklessly into the Scottish ranks, to be brought down and killed by a spear thrust. In his blind anger he had omitted to put on the surcoat with his golden chevrons that would have identified him as a desirable prisoner for whom a great ransom might be demanded.

His knights and troopers had followed him, but fell into disorder when they lost their leader. Most of the Berkeley party, as always fighting alongside the de Clares, were killed or taken prisoner. Thomas, his younger son and several of his knights were captured. From the early disaster the English army did not recover; the archers who had won so many victories were cut down by the Scottish light cavalry; English knights could make no impression on the spearmen. Their horses floundered in the marsh; the bannerets lost control of their companies; the army became a disordered mass.

Maurice de Berkeley was fighting in the royal bodyguard. When defeat had become certain a group of knights gathered around Edward and fought their way with him from the battlefield. The king behaved bravely, using his battle-axe to force a passage. He was almost captured when some Scots recognised the royal liveries and coat of arms, but he managed to break through.

More survivors of the battle joined them. With five hundred horsemen Edward rode by day and night to Dunbar, where the castle was still held by the English. By his side was Maurice de Berkeley, as he had ridden in more fortunate days to the siege of Caerlaverock. From Dunbar they sailed to Berwick and safety.

So ended Edward's first and last appearance as a commander in a pitched battle fought by two large armies. He had neither the generalship nor the self-discipline that his father had acquired by long apprenticeship to war. Scores of men of rank were left prisoners in Scottish hands; perhaps a quarter of the barons had been killed in combat, smothered in the marsh or drowned by the weight of their armour in the river Forth. There were many Gloucestershire men among the infantry slaughtered on the battlefield or hunted down later; some reached home as ragged starving refugees.

For the Berkeleys the Bannockburn defeat was a disaster greater than anything the family had experienced. Up to that moment war had added to their prosperity. Now Thomas and many of his knights were prisoners and much ransom money had to be found. The war horses of which he was so proud had been killed or captured. Only Maurice was free to rebuild the family fortunes.

Thomas's second son, also named Thomas, was released on parole so that he could go to Berkeley to raise the money. A heavy burden was laid on the Berkeley manors; it took a year to collect enough to buy old Thomas's release. Ransoms had to be paid in cash. Coin was hard to come by in medieval times; sudden need for large sums created difficulty even for the wealthiest families. Not until three years after the battle had the freedom of the last knights been bought. Old Thomas must have felt the disgrace keenly, coming as it did near the end of a long military career.

CHAPTER THREE

A TUMULT OF BARONS

'A ranker rout of rebels never was'.
MARLOWE: EDWARD II.

The defeat at Bannockburn was a catastrophe from which English military power did not recover for nearly twenty years. Five hundred barons, knights and squires had been taken prisoner and an even greater number killed. Adding to the difficulties of the government, the next year was one of excessive rainfall that ruined the harvest, led to the loss of livestock through disease and brought famine to the peasantry. The following year was not much better. We do not know exactly how this affected the Berkeley manors but it may partly explain the long delay before all the ransom money was paid.

Edward's leadership was discredited. He had to hand over the effective command of the army to Thomas of Lancaster; co-operation between him and the king was impossible, nor did many of the barons trust the earl. Naturally he was no more successful than Edward had been.

The barons remained divided. Some still supported the king, others remained implacably hostile, whilst a middle group tried to find a solution to the problem of government that would restore unity. Then came the rise to power of the two Despensers, father and son, both named Hugh. The younger one replaced Gaveston in the king's affections, arousing the same antagonisms. The barons made the same accusations about the new favourite: that he was homosexual and a fortune hunter. So the political scene became even more troubled.

The Berkeleys remained aloof from these quarrels and intrigues. Thomas was out of action for a year as a prisoner of war; it took him another two before he recovered his knights; until then he was fully occupied in

24

Gloucestershire. Maurice, however, stood high in the king's estimation, not as a court favourite but as a reliable fighting man, apparently not much interested in politics. In 1315 Edward appointed him governor and garrison commander of the key frontier town of Berwick. The usual company of Berkeley knights and relatives went with him; they saw much action against Scottish raiding parties and acquitted themselves well. The royal citation at the end of this service says that Maurice undertook it "out of his own goodwill", which sounds as though he was a volunteer for a difficult job that no one wanted. All the same, he was never paid for doing it. Fifteen years later his son was credited with the sum owing, to be set against what *he* owed the Crown.

After a year at Berwick Maurice was appointed Justiciar of South and West Wales, with special responsibility for recruiting men for the king's forces. Each year he led them up to the border. In the meantime Berwick had been lost; in 1318 a large army tried to recover it. That year three generations of Berkeleys were in the field together; old Lord Thomas, now in his seventy-third year, his sons Maurice and Thomas, and his twenty-one year old grandson, another Thomas. It was the veteran's last campaign, like so many recent ones, disappointing. Berwick was not retaken; Edward and the Despensers were blamed.

At this point in the story the Marcher lords of the Welsh border begin to play a more important part. Bannockburn had left another problem. Gilbert de Clare, the young Earl of Gloucester killed in the battle, was the Marcher who ruled most of Glamorgan; the Bohuns of Hereford were the most powerful lords of the middle March; the Mortimers of the lands to the north. After some delay Edward allotted the de Clare inheritance to Gilbert's three brothers-in-law, the younger Despenser and the barons Amory and d'Audley. Though Despenser got the larger share the settlement aroused no objections, but by bringing him into the March it held the seeds of later trouble.

Many other English barons held smaller, yet valuable lands in the March. One such was John Giffard, "le Rych", of Brimpsfield Castle on the Cotswolds; the head of another family linked by marriage to the Berkeleys. All these Marchers, greater or lesser, exercised almost independent powers in their frontier fiefs; all were extremely vigilant and assertive about their rights and privileges.

The Berkeleys were not Marcher lords but they had always been closely associated with the de Clares and the Mortimers. Now Maurice married as his second wife an aunt of Gilbert, thus coming into possession of some de Clare manors. Of greater consequence was the marriage of his son, the younger Thomas, to the twelve year old Margaret Mortimer, daugher of Roger Mortimer of Wigmore Castle in Herefordshire. Thus was forged a baronial link that involved the Berkeleys in Marcher quarrels and eventually in the events that led to the deposition and death of Edward II.

But in 1320 Maurice Berkeley was the most trusted servant of the crown. In that year he reached the high point of his career when Edward sent him out to Bordeaux as Seneschal, that is, as Governor and Commander-in-chief of Gascony and the Duchy of Aquitaine, one of the grandest and most lucrative appointments in the gift of the king. He received at once the sume of £100 for the expenses of the journey and a salary of £2,000 a year which would be paid out of the revenues of that rich province.

The population of Aquitaine was then more than six hundred thousand and Bordeaux was a larger city than London. The province was an important market for English broadcloth and leather goods and for English grain. From Bordeaux came dye stuffs, olive oil and the products of the south of France and great quantities of wine. The prosperity of Bristol was based on this trade.

In February Maurice sailed from Bristol taking with him his sons Thomas and Maurice the younger, many other Berkeley relatives and household knights and companions in battle like Sir John Maltravers, Sir Thomas Gournay and his neighbour Thomas de Bradestone. He was going to a post that called for diplomatic skill since Aquitaine was a dukedom held as a fief from the French king so Maurice could sometimes be required to attend the court and Parliament of France. His judicial duties obliged him to preside over assizes at least once each year in the four parts of the duchy to settle feudal disputes and ensure peace and good order.

Administrative talent had to be matched by military competence. Along the extensive frontiers of the province were many truculent, semi-independent barons, some owing allegiance to Edward, some to the king of France and some others to both kings for different parts of their estates, and all of them quick to assert and to extend their feudal rights and privileges by force when they saw a prospect of successful rebellion. No doubt the battle-hardened Berkeleys relished the prospect of some action against trouble-makers. Though the job was demanding, the opportunities for rich pickings were attractive.

Unfortunately, something went wrong in Aquitaine. That autumn Edward II came to Amiens to do homage to the French king for the duchy. Maurice of course was there in attendance. Presumably complaints were made by the French about his administration of the province for shortly afterwards Edward sent Hugh Despenser the elder to Bordeaux "to enquire into all offices and misdemeanours". His report has not survived, so we do not know what it was all about. Perhaps some scrap of evidence that would explain the affair lies in some forgotten archive in France or England but this is not likely. Whatever the trouble, Maurice and all his attendant Berkeleys were back in England in February 1321.

Maurice returned to find the Marches in an uproar. The Despensers, not satisfied with their share of the de Clare lands, were extending their hold on South Wales and Herefordshire at the expense of Lords Audley and Damory. Even more rashly they were encroaching on Mortimer lands farther north. Under cover of local tournaments, often the scene of baronial plotting, Roger Mortimer, his uncle Roger Mortimer of Chirk, the Bohuns, Audley, Damory and John Giffard were meeting in conference. Edward wrote to them optimistically, ordering them "not to discuss the affairs of the kingdom".

Maurice himself was alarmed to find that the elder Despenser had been given custody of the city and castle of Bristol. This seemed to be a threat to his very valuable manor of Bedminster and Redcliffe, just outside the city wall. More disturbing still was a rumour that the younger Despenser was to be created Earl of Gloucester. The father had been responsible for Maurice's dismissal from the governorship of Aquitaine; now it seemed that father and son were threatening his inheritance.

The "trusty and well-beloved cousin" of the king who had been sent to Bordeaux now took the road leading to rebellion. Filled with anger about the Despensers he followed the example of the Marchers, gathering the Gloucestershire men who had so often answered the Berkeley call to arms. Edward tried to assert royal authority by coming to Gloucester, ordering the western sheriffs to suppress all unlawful assemblies. With Maurice and John Giffard in arms, there was not much that the poor sheriff of Gloucestershire could do about this, especially as the force with the king was not strong enough to confront the offenders.

Edward's next move was to call Parliament to him at Gloucester to "discuss and advise" what should be done about the armed gatherings in Wales and the Marches. Maurice and old Lord Thomas ignored the

Edward II. Detail from the effigy in Gloucester Cathedral. Note the graffiti. There were vandals in 1709.

summons, as did most of the other barons. The king wrote to the Berkeleys complaining about the warlike preparations being made in their manors, warning them to keep the peace on pain of confiscation of their lands. His only action was to seize Audley's small Forest of Dean castle of St. Briavel's, thereby still further angering the Marchers. Realising that he was outnumbered, Edward was obliged to withdraw to Wallingford, not daring to attack either Berkeley or Brimpsfield. Another letter to the Berkeleys condemned the "evil-minded persons going up and down the kingdom, sowing lies and raising people into tumults". See that you repress all such rumours and maintain the peace!

These were wasted, ineffective words. Maurice's answer was to march with all his allies and retainers to Hereford, where the Marcher lords had gathered; altogether a formidable force, not less than eight hundred knights and troopers, with light horsemen and infantry. Their proclaimed object was to destroy Despenser power in the border country, not to rebel against Edward; they marched with the royal banner flying beside their own as a somewhat dubious sign of their loyalty. Old Lord Thomas was not with them; he was on his deathbed in Berkeley Castle.

The barons' first attack was on the town and castle of Newport, taken after a destructive four day siege. Raiding parties then scattered over Monmouth and Glamorgan; granges and farms were plundered or burnt on more than twenty Despenser manors. As always in civil commotions many innocent people suffered loss at the hands of opportunist freebooters, who even robbed lands belonging to monastic houses. Some prominent Despenser vassals and many of their Welsh tenants were murdered; hundreds of prisoners were held to ransom. As these were fellow subjects of the king this was nothing more or less than kidnapping.

The account of the barons' depredations tells of the seizure of armour and food supplies to the value of more than £2,000, of breeding mares and stallions and over a thousand head of cattle. No doubt Maurice reflected that this was much more rewarding than campaigns in Galloway. Significantly, the marauders made a point of burning "evidences", the legal documents giving possession of the manors to the Despensers.

"Contrary to all usage" the barons carried away the plunder and divided it among themselves. It was a brief and violent affair, over in a fortnight. The force used was overwhelming; after the fall of Newport the Despensers' men had neither the will nor the military strength to defend their castles and manor houses. Thousands of tenants had to renounce their allegiance and swear on the Gospels that they would perform all due services to the true heirs of Gilbert de Clare. Amory and Audley had not only regained their own manors, they had taken many others granted to the Despensers by Edward.

The marcher barons, flushed with their success, now carried the attack to the Despensers' English manors. One column dealt with Cheshire and Yorkshire, another moved into the Midlands; Maurice de Berkeley and his allies swept through Wiltshire, Hampshire and Dorset. They had a stroke of luck at Marlborough, finding in the castle a great store of Despenser wealth, some £6,000 worth of wool and cloth, crosses of gold and ivory and other valuable objects. Altogether the loot from the English manors was reckoned at £38,000. The record lists, probably with some exaggeration, 28,000 sheep, 1,000 oxen, 1,000 cows with calves, 2,000 swine and large quantities of bacon, beef and mutton from the larders. Game preserves were broken into and deer slaughtered.

Faced with these disorders, Edward summoned Parliament. The rebels, including Maurice, first rode north to confer with Thomas of Lancaster and concert their actions. Each baron then returned home to gather his men. When they came to Westminster they brought with them thousands of supporters in battle array. Thomas de Berkeley knew nothing of this; he died two days after Parliament met.

From a position of strength the barons told the king that he must disinherit and exile the Despensers. Should he refuse, they would renounce their homage and "as men without a ruler or judge take their own vengeance" on the hated favourites. Edward could not resist. Not only was he compelled to send the Despensers away, he had to grant four hundred and fifty pardons to the barons for their "homicides, robberies, trespasses and felonies". Either by oversight or deliberately these were not enrolled as acts of Parliament, so they proved valueless when political fortune swung the other way.

Unexpectedly, this swing began almost at once. The Marcher barons having won their victory simply went home without taking any steps to make it secure. Many other barons felt that the rebels had carried violence too far. The Despenser lands had been conveyed to them by the king in due legal form; refusal to respect this had set a dangerous example.

Support, perhaps not so much for the king as for the institution of monarchy, increased astonishingly in the next few weeks. In October when the queen was refused entrance to Leeds Castle in Kent, the home of

Badlesmere, one of the rebel barons, Edward was able to besiege it with a powerful force. It was quickly taken and a dozen defenders executed. As soon as the Marchers heard what was happening they mobilised quickly, advancing as far as Richmond-on-Thames. But Thomas of Lancaster made no move to join them. Realising that Edward's army was too powerful for them to attack they retired again to the west.

It was Edward's turn to take the initiative. In one of his occasional bursts of energetic action he recalled the Despensers from exile; the sheriffs of the southern counties were ordered to meet him in Cirencester with their infantry. A letter to Maurice de Berkeley warned him against associating with the rebels, but he was already in Warwickshire leading a marauding body that was responsible for "divers murders and burnings".

From Cirencester Edward moved on to Gloucester, seizing several small Marcher strongholds across the Severn. John Giffard, from his strategically placed castle of Brimpsfield, near the Cirencester–Gloucester road, was the first to take up arms against the king. He boldly and rashly attacked and plundered the royal baggage train, before leaving to join the rebels. For this exploit his manors were confiscated, he was declared an enemy of the king and orders were given to the sheriff of Gloucester to demolish his massive castle—a task that occupied him for some years.

Almost all the knights of Gloucestershire had now joined Mortimer and the Bohuns. Edward therefore seized their lands: the Berkeley manors, those of Maurice's allies, John Maltravers, Nigel de Kingscote, Thomas de Bradestone and about fifty others. A royal constable was placed in Berkeley Castle; two commissioners were ordered to find out by all ways and means the jewels, plate and other goods belonging to Maurice and seize them for the Crown.

The wily Maurice had anticipated this. Before taking the field he had sent his most treasured possessions to the abbey of St. Augustine in Bristol for safe keeping: two coffers of ivory plated with silver, gilt with gold, eighteen silver vessels, a vial of precious oil, a piece of wood of the Holy Cross, divers pearls, emeralds, sapphires and two crosses of gold and two books. Despite the search, there they remained for years until they were delivered to his heir.

The rebel barons, now gathered in strength around Hereford, still received no support from Lancaster. The king seems to have lost control of the bridges at Gloucester but, determined to cross the Severn again, he marched northwards to Tewkesbury and Worcester. The bridges there were also strongly held by the barons so he moved on to Bridgnorth. Here the Mortimers offered powerful resistance; part of the town was burnt but the bridge was still denied him.

At this moment Sir Griffyth Lloyd, formerly a gentleman of Edward's household, made a decisive intervention. At the head of a force that included men from the garrisons of the royal castles in north Wales, and Welshmen who much preferred Edward of Caernarvon to the Mortimers and their like, he captured Chirk, the castle of the elder Mortimer and advanced into Shropshire. With the Welsh in arms behind them, overrunning their lands, the rebel barons panicked; a sudden collapse followed as their army disintegrated. In the confusion Edward was able to cross at Shrewsbury.

The end came quickly. By the last days of January all fighting along the border had ended; castles everywhere surrendered to the king. Returning by way of Gloucester, Edward found there Maurice de Berkeley, Lord Audley and the two Mortimers, who had taken advantage of a safe conduct to give themselves up. He "received them into his grace" and placed them under arrest. The Mortimers were sent to the Tower of London, Maurice and Audley to Wallingford Castle. On the whole, their followers were leniently treated.

Not all the rebels surrendered so easily. Maurice's sons, the hot-headed Thomas and Maurice the younger "filled with heat and rage by their father's imprisonment, whirled about into those counties where the Despensers had lands, wasting, burning, pulling down, destroying and carrying away without measure or mercy whatsoever goods and chattels they could find in the counties of Oxford, Buckingham and others".

Meanwhile, de Bohun, Mowbray, John Giffard and other rebel barons had evaded the royal army and joined Lancaster, who at last had mobilised his considerable forces. Edward at once marched against them. The rebel army was completely destroyed at Boroughbridge in Yorkshire. Lancaster surrendered, was taken to Pontefract Castle and denounced by the king before a group of magnates who sentenced him to death. After eight years Edward had his revenge for the murder of Piers Gaveston.

Savage retribution followed. Five more rebel barons were hanged at Pontefract, two more at York. Other leaders were sent to cities throughout England and Wales where they were well known, that their deaths might make known the extent of the king's victory. There were executions in London, Bristol, Canterbury, Cardiff and Windsor. John Giffard was brought to Gloucester, there to be tried, sentenced, drawn and hanged. He was the last of his line; his castle at Brimpsfield was utterly demolished; for long afterwards its heaps of stone provided building material for Cotswold farms and cottages.

Up and down the country knights whose names have often not survived remained hanging on the gallows on which they paid the penalty for following their masters into rebellion. Edward had not so far in his life shown himself to be vindictive, cruel or bloodthirsty; all this butchery seems to be out of character. In all likelihood it was the work of the Despensers. Certainly they were blamed for it. Some thirty barons had been hanged; for the moment and for some time to come the opposition to the king had been destroyed.

No Berkeley lost his life on the gallows in the great purge of 1322. Although they had been prominent in the attack on the Despenser lands, it was not treason to despoil the manors of a fellow magnate—merely a disturbance of the peace, no matter how much blood was shed or plunder carried away. Of course, in that ever-memorable phrase, "except for the common man", who, should he steal his lord's horse or cow and be detected, would certainly find himself on his lordship's private gallows.

Luckily for Maurice and most of his allies they had surrendered before Boroughbridge. Their involvement in the minor clashes over the Severn bridges was overlooked, presumably because of the safe-conduct. Nor had Maurice's two sons joined Lancaster though they went on looting Despenser property. An enquiry into their depredations in Oxfordshire lists the usual seizures of plate and valuables, hundreds of cattle, thousands of sheep, the killing of deer and a hundred swans.

Thomas was caught after the issue of many orders to keepers of the peace to search for and arrest him, but young Maurice evaded them and remained free all through the years of Despenser rule, living secretly in the homes of friends and relatives and hiding in monasteries until it was safe for him to appear again.

Sir John Maltravers, Sir Thomas Gournay and a few other Berkeley knights had ill-advisedly gone to Boroughbridge. More fortunate than most who had done so they slipped away to the continent. There was no difficulty about earning a living. A free-lance knight could always find employment in the endless fighting on the eastern borders of Prussia or in the baronial wars that continually disturbed the peace of western Europe.

Most fortunate of all (or perhaps more clever) was Thomas de

Bradestone, whose family had for generations held two small manors from the Berkeleys in return for military service. This young man "so wrought that for £100 he redeemed his life and lands, finding sureties and taking oath for his good behaviour towards the king". Then, two years later "wittily winding himself into favour", he obtained the custody of Kingswood Chase, a royal hunting ground that extended from Berkeley almost to Bristol. I suspect that during these years he was helping the younger Maurice de Berkeley, perhaps secreting him in his little manor house at Bradestone. At all events, they afterwards became life-long friends and companions in war.

CHAPTER FOUR

THE WHEEL OF CHANGE

'By force and against the laws of England and
accroaching to yourself royal power, you
counselled the king to disinherit and undo his lieges.'
INDICTMENT OF HUGH DESPENSER THE ELDER,
1326

The Despensers had emerged from the brief and bloody struggle with all political power in their hands. That two men, not members of a baronial family, were able to reach such a position so quickly was made possible by Edward's affection for the younger one, but it would not have happened if the barons had not been so disunited.

Able though the Despensers were, they were outsiders who failed completely to understand the depth of feeling that led the Marcher lords to rebel. This lack of comprehension of baronial psychology led them to go on adding to their castles, manors and offices of profit until, between them, they owned a great part of the inheritance of Thomas of Lancaster, the Mortimers and the Bohuns. As Maurice de Berkeley had feared, the elder Hugh took over Bedminster and his other Somerset manors as well as Berkeley Castle and its dependent lands. The dispossessed families were in no position to protest but the Despensers' greed and domination of the king aroused resentment and anger in the minds even of barons who had remained loyal during the rebellion.

Failure to deal effectively with Scottish raids was, as always, a cause of baronial unrest. Robert Bruce continued to ravage the north. Edward and the Despensers led one disastrous march into Scotland that ended with an inglorious retreat with Bruce hard on their heels. Edward himself was almost captured; Queen Isabel, left to shift for herself, made a hazardous escape by sea. The best that the Despensers could do was to arrange a thirteen years truce, which disgusted the barons.

Whilst the Despensers enjoyed the fruits of his manors, Maurice de Berkeley was shut up in Wallingford Castle, an immense fortification surrounded by a treble moat and an outer wall nine feet thick, On a central mound stood the massive keep in which the prisoners were confined. Maurice and Audley were not subjected to very rigorous conditions. They were allowed to receive visitors; the constable of the castle was friendly. No doubt he had it in mind that their roles might be reversed by a sudden change of fortune. For a year they lived pleasantly enough, perhaps swapping stories of campaigns they had shared.

Some Berkeley neighbours and friends then hatched a plot to rescue Maurice. Three of his knights arrived in Wallingford with a group of retainers; this would arouse no comment as the town was on the main road from Gloucester to London with several inns for travellers. At the same time Robert de Wauton, one of Maurice's squires, and three companions came to the castle with a few home comforts for his master—perhaps Gloucestershire wine and venison. He was a regular visitor so was admitted without question. That evening Maurice invited the constable to dine with him. The provision must have been ample, since guards, doorkeepers and watchmen were all invited to the banquet.

When wine and ale had put the constable and his officers into a pleasantly relaxed mood, Robert and his friends leapt up from the table demanding, at point of sword, the keys of the castle. The guards having most unwisely come unarmed to the feast were obliged to hand them over, though one would have thought that a dozen or more men of spirit could have dealt with four intruders armed only with sword and dagger, provided, of course, that they were sober enough, which they may not have been. As it was they allowed themselves to be detained while Robert admitted some of the rescue party who were waiting at a private, unguarded gate; enough to give them control of part, though not all, of the castle.

The plan then began to go wrong. A boy at the main gate, suspecting that something unusual was happening, ran to the mayor. He at once ordered that the bells should be rung to summon the townsmen. They reacted with enthusiasm, adding to the din by shouting and blowing horns. Within minutes guards had been posted at every castle gate.

It had been planned to get Maurice and Audley away at dawn. Instead, in the morning came the sheriff of Berkshire with reinforcements, besieging the castle until the elder Despenser (him, again!) arrived with an overwhelming force, whereupon the castle gates were thrown open. The conspirators were arrested, but Maurice was found sitting in his cell, blandly denying that he had any part in the affair.

The three knights were tried and let off with a fine of 500 marks apiece, but the unfortunate squire Robert was executed, judged guilty of gross deception. Understandably alarmed, the government ordered constables of castles to take stricter precautions against the release of prisoners, whose imprisonment now became less pleasant. Maurice's health began to decline; for a man whose life had been so full of activity—war, the tournament, hunting, political adminstration—life must indeed have been irksome.

Another plot was hatched to release the two Mortimers from the Tower; possibly organised by Adam Orleton, Bishop of Hereford. The feast of St. Peter ad Vincula, 1st August 1323 was appropriately chosen for the attempt, prepared with careful attention to timing and detail. Two London merchants, John de Gisors and Richard de Bettoyne, staged a feast day banquet for the constable and his officers. It is surprising that the invitation was accepted, after the affair at Wallingford, but one must assume that the merchants were well known to the constable.

On this occasion the plotters brought in a plentiful supply of drugged wine, the potency of which is revealed in a report made six days later that the constable was still unfit for duty. As soon as the guests were overcome by the wine, a hole was cut in the wall of the younger Mortimer's cell, enabling him to crawl out into the palace kitchen. Presumably the cooks were also under the influence as Mortimer was able to climb out on to the roof and drop to the inner courtyard. Here one of the plotters was waiting with a rope ladder to help him reach the outer courtyard.

Climbing over the outer wall by the same rope ladder, Mortimer dropped to the river bank where two boatmen were waiting to row him over to the Surrey bank. All this was done without the alarm being raised. Across the river were men and horses. The little party rode swiftly by devious ways to Portchester. By the time messengers reached sheriffs and port officers Roger Mortimer was aboard ship and on his way to France. All had gone without a hitch, except that the elder Mortimer was too weak to make the hazardous climb. He died soon afterwards in his cell, far from his castle in the border hills.

Roger Mortimer made his way to the castle of St. Omer in Picardy, a rallying point for the growing number of exiles from Despenser rule. As the only really important "contrariant" to escape, Roger was their natural leader. The proscribed rebels were a tough and revengeful lot who had nothing to lose. The Berkeley knight, John Maltravers, knew that as long as Edward was king he would never see his manors again. Sir Robert Walkelare, who had killed the constable of Corfe Castle when escaping, knew that he would end on the scaffold if he returned alone to England. There were many more of this kind in Germany and the Low Countries.

After a time Mortimer went to Paris, offering his services to Charles IV, Queen Isabel's brother, now king of France. He was given the welcome that a competent knight always received. Knighthood was international; it was common for a vassal who had quarrelled with his lord to give allegiance to another; no one thought the worse of him. Froissart's Chronicles are full of such examples. Language was no barrier; Norman-French was still the tongue of the English aristocracy. Though French nobles were supercilious about the accent, it could be understood.

Meanwhile, in England dissatisfaction with Edward and the Despensers continued to grow among bishops and barons. In 1324 the bodies of the condemned rebels were still hanging on the gallows. Public opinion was so shocked by this that Parliament petitioned the king that they should be taken down and given Christian burial. When this had been done the tombs of Thomas of Lancaster and others were turned into shrines by the common people. Pilgrims began to report an impressive number of miracles performed by the departed to demonstrate the injustice of their fate. Miracles, of course, were almost everyday occurrences in medieval life; the Virgin putting in frequent appearances in western Europe whilst cripples were made whole and the blind to see with a frequency greater than in New Testament times.

In the summer of 1324 a new factor changed the situation: an open breach between Edward and his queen. The king had increasingly neglected her; on three occasions when she had been in danger of capture by the Scots he had left her to escape as best she could. Now, according to a letter she wrote, she had been replaced in his affections by the younger Despenser, his homosexual lover, and her marriage had become a mere facade.

Isabel's opportunity came when the question of homage for Aquitaine was raised again by Charles IV. She was sent to Paris to restore friendly relations between the two kings. It was agreed that the young Edward, her eldest son, should be created Duke of Aquitaine so that he could join his mother in France and do homage for the duchy. This was done to everyone's satisfaction, but Isabel would neither return to England nor allow her son to do so.

At the French court she had met Roger Mortimer, who must already have been known to her. They shared a common hatred of the Despensers, but Isabel was strongly attracted to him as a man. He was now about forty, in every way a contrast to the husband she had left. Proud and wealthy, skilled in the use of arms, a man used to making decisions, he was a fine specimen of his class. As for Isabel, she was now the "femme de trente ans", at that dangerous age when a mature woman may begin to look critically at the man she married and with interest at a man she did not.

From Paris they began to organise support among the barons and bishops in England. Messages were sent to exiled knights all over Europe. Charles IV, shocked by the way they openly lived together, would have no part in their invasion plan.

They moved to the court of William II, Count of Hainault, Holland and Zeeland. He had already been sounded; a bargain was soon struck. A marriage was arranged between Prince Edward and William's daughter Philippa. Her dowry would be a contingent of Flemish soldiers and the ships to transport them to England. Isabel helped to finance the project by pawning her jewels. From all directions the exiled rebels of 1322 made their way to Dordrecht.

In England the summer months of 1326 were uneasy with rumours of invasion. The Despensers made futile efforts to put the kingdom into a state of defence. A thousand pounds were offered for the head of Roger Mortimer; it is not surprising that there were no volunteers for what would have been an extremely hazardous mission.

In early autumn the king's half-brother, Thomas, Earl of Norfolk, a party to the plot, began to move his retainers to the neighbourhood of Ipswich, closing it to the outside world. On 26th September nine Flemish ships crammed with soldiers appeared in the river Orwell. The invaders disembarked with all their equipment, commandeering horses from all the farms around. Then Isabel and her son landed, with Edward, Earl of Kent, who had joined her in Paris. Altogether the queen's army numbered only 1,500 men, half of them Hainaulters.

No sheriff or magnate challenged the invaders. They marched unopposed to Cambridge, strengthened there by the arrival of Henry of Lancaster, brother of the late earl, and barons from the Midlands. Edward was in the Tower of London, but when it became clear that the citizens were dangerously hostile he left for Bristol with only the knights and archers of the royal bodyguard. As soon as he had gone the city broke into open rebellion.

Isabel by now was at Oxford. Prompted no doubt by Mortimer, she had sent an order to Pevensey for Thomas de Berkeley's release; he at once joined her. The invasion came a few weeks too late for Thomas's father. Maurice had died in Wallingford; he was only forty-six, and in the five years since he succeeded his father he had held his inheritance for only five months, for almost all of which he had been in rebellion.

Leaving the elder Despenser in charge of Bristol, Edward rode to Gloucester with an ever-diminishing escort. Hearing of the queen's approach he spent only two days with abbot Thokey at St. Peter's before moving on to Cardiff. From there he sent an order to Thomas de Bradestone to recruit men-at-arms and archers for the defence of Berkeley Castle. No doubt Bradestone knew that his master had arrived at Oxford so he quickly switched his allegiance, placed a garrison in the castle to hold it for the queen and led the rest to join her at Gloucester. To that city came the retainers of the Marcher lords, eager to avenge the executions of 1322.

Mortimer decided that they must first make sure of Bristol. The invaders, now a much larger army, marched out of the south gate of Gloucester along the old Roman highway beneath the Cotswold edge. Thomas de Berkeley was with them, but he was careful not to turn aside to enter his castle, still technically in the hands of the Crown, until the necessary formalities had been completed.

Bristol was easily taken. The castle held out for a few days, but the elder Despenser fell into the hands of those who had lost friends and relatives in the butchery that followed Boroughbridge. Mortimer and Isabel took a savage revenge. The old man was brought before a court of magnates, his crimes listed without right of reply and sentence of death passed.

At the High Cross the fifteen year old Prince Edward sat between his mother and her lover, surrounded by grim and silent barons, to watch the cruel spectacle. The old earl in his golden and red surcoat was dragged feet first across the cobbles at the tail of a horse, strung up on the gallows, half strangled, taken down and disembowelled, his entrails burnt before him, his body hung up again after his head had been cut off, to be sent for exhibition at Winchester. Who can tell what the boy thought of this? Ruthless as the future Edward III could be in war, his long reign was remarkably free from these barbarities.

The grisly business finished in Bristol, Mortimer and Isabel returned to Gloucester. From Berkeley records we get a glimpse of what the passage of armed strangers, obliged often to live off the country, meant to the medieval peasant. The reeves of Slimbridge and Hurst complained that the Earl of Leicester's men took their hens, geese and ducks, depriving them of the poultry that would have given them meat and eggs in the winter. They do not charge the earl's men with stealing; only with "alienating" these things. At Wotton-under-Edge the Earl of Kent's men broke into barns and took oats; at Ham cattle and swine were carried off; Cam and Coaley were plundered by the Flemish contingent. These were all Berkeley manors; no doubt the same thing happened all along the route. There must also have been a good deal of petty thieving, violence and molestation of simple country people by ill-disciplined soldiers against whom there was no remedy. They disappeared beyond all possibility of tracing them, even if anyone had been interested in seeing that peasants received justice.

By the end of October Isabel was at Hereford, which became her headquarters. Every day spies brought news of the king; she soon knew that he had left Cardiff, accompanied now only by Hugh Despenser and a pitifully small band of servants and officials. Henry of Lancaster, his cousin, and William de la Zouche (Thomas de Berkeley's uncle) were sent to arrest him.

Their mission was neither long nor difficult. They found Edward in the abbey at Neath, where he had taken shelter. Despenser escaped for the moment but was taken a few days later, hiding in a wood near Llantrisant. The king was brought to Monmouth, where Bishop Orleton demanded and received the Great Seal of England. Possession of this enabled Isabel to call a Parliament.

It was decided that Henry of Lancaster should take Edward to his castle of Kenilworth by a route that would avoid all contact with the queen's party. Hugh Despenser was brought to Hereford so that Isabel could exact a cruel vengeance. Every indignity was heaped upon him. Next day he was brought before the queen; a list of his alleged misdeeds was read and he was sentenced to death.

He was executed with even greater barbarity than that inflicted upon his father at Bristol. Such brutal spectacles became not uncommon in the later Middle Ages. They began in England with the murder of Gaveston,

Thomas of Lancaster and the execution of the Boroughbridge rebels, but the treatment of the Despensers reached a new high level of cruelty, hitherto unknown in England. The execution of a man of high rank, which did not happen every day, was an event to be savoured by the mob with greater relish than the hanging of a common thief. Ordinary people whose life was indeed "nasty, brutish and short" and subject to the chances of war, famine and plague were consoled in their misfortunes by the assurance that the mighty, too, could be struck down by the random blows of fate.

We should not be too ready to condemn them for the eagerness with which they flocked to such spectacles. These crude gratifications have been replaced in our own day by a more domestic enjoyment of stories of torture, perversion and violence, the stock themes of a thousand paper-backs, and, in a somewhat more discreet form, of film and television.

As for those who inflicted these savage punishments, though the Victorians could with good conscience regard them with disgust and horror as products of the age of barbarism, we can hardly take the same superior view, now that our own century has seen the murder, degradation and torture of human beings on an infinitely greater scale.

The capture of the king ended military operations, such as they had been. In eight weeks the Despenser regime had been demolished without the fighting of a single battle. Isabel and Mortimer set out on a triumphant march to London, where they were given an enthusiastic welcome. They then spent Christmas "happily and mirthfully" at Wallingford, whilst Edward, separated from his friends by their deaths, lay in prison.

Perhaps, however, the festivities at Wallingford were clouded by some feeling of uncertainty. Edward was still king of England; there were no precedents for depriving God's anointed of his throne. Nor was it likely that all the barons, much less all the bishops, would agree to his dethronement.

Earls and barons, bishops and abbots, knights of the shire and burgesses gathered at Westminster in January, yet all knew that without the presence of the king it was not a Parliament. So two bishops were sent to Edward to invite him to come to Westminster. With no one to advise him, he refused. It was a mistake. Had he come to Parliament, many of the barons would have been ready to work out a compromise settlement.

The rest of the business was carefully stage-managed. There were demonstrations by the London mob, followed by three days of oath-taking when every member of the assembly swore to support the queen and her son to the death. A delegation was then sent to Kenilworth to demand Edward's abdication. Our knowledge of what happened there comes from a single knight, Sir Thomas de la More, who was present in attendance on the delegation. He told his recollections to a chronicler some time afterwards; they may not have been entirely accurate.

No time was wasted. Two bishops saw Edward at once. They found him in a state of collapse, clothed in a long black robe, broken in spirit. Bishop Orleton, the spokesman, told him that if he would abdicate in favour of his son he would be allowed a dignified retirement. If he refused, Parliament would choose another king, not of the royal line. If this threat was actually made it was pure bluff; Parliament would never have done this; the one thing on which all would agree was that the king of England must be of the blood royal.

Edward agreed to meet the full delegation publicly. Orleton loudly and arrogantly repeated the threat; the king, in tears, replied that he was saddened by the knowledge that his subjects no longer desired him to rule, but that he would abdicate if his son's accession was assured.

Next day, in the same hall, Sir William Trussell, speaking in the name of the earls and barons of England, renounced all homage and allegiance. The steward of Edward's household, in a dramatic gesture, broke his staff of office, throwing the pieces clattering to the floor as a sign that the royal establishment was disbanded. The delegation then returned to London, leaving the ex-king to his bitter memories and regrets.

The new reign, it was announced, began on 25th January, 1327; the coronation of the boy king followed on the first day of February. At such short notice it must have been a comparatively simple ceremony; dominated by the grim and powerful presence of Roger Mortimer, who at the coronation of Edward II had presented the alb and tunicle and now had deprived him of his kingdom.

Again, we do not know what thoughts were in the mind of the boy king on whose head the crown was placed and before whom the earls and barons who had rebelled against his father knelt in homage. We do not know if his thoughts turned to the unhappy man at Kenilworth, or indeed if he had enough affection for his father to care about his fate. We do know that in the next few years he grew rapidly into manhood and political maturity; it can be safely assumed that he had no illusions about what was happening around him.

CHAPTER FIVE

THE CAPTIVE KING

'Now lords, consider well, kings, dukes, counts,
prelates, all men of noble lineage and power, how
fickle are the chances of this world."
JEAN FROISSART: CHRONICLES

For two months after his deposition Edward remained at Kenilworth in the custody of his cousin Henry, a sincerely religious man who had not been contaminated by the intrigue, treachery and bloodshed of the times. Kenilworth, with a compassionate gaoler, was not an unpleasant place. Edward was not shut in a prison cell; he had his own personal attendants, was treated with respect and allowed to move freely around in the seven acres enclosed by the castle walls. Yet it was a dismal and unhappy time for him, suddenly deprived of all authority, deserted by many whom he had thought to be his friends and cut off from those still loyal to him.

His feelings are expressed in a poem said to have been written by him at this time:

> In winter woe befell me,
> By cruel fortune threatened
> My life now lies a ruin.
> Once was I feared and dreaded
> But now all men despise me
> And call me a crownless king,
> A laughing stock to all.

Other verses show him turning to prayer, seeking consolation in his deep misfortune. By temperament always cheerful and optimistic, long accustomed to crises which somehow had always resolved themselves

44

leaving him unharmed, the abruptness of his fall from power had reduced him to despair.

Early in 1327 Roger Mortimer received some alarming news of disturbances in the Midlands, particularly in the country around Kenilworth. Dunsmore, then a stretch of wild heathland to the south of Coventry, was the centre of this unrest. Stephen Dunhead, lord of the manor of Dunchurch, had gathered around him a mob of determined and reckless men. Roving bands of this kind, engaged in deer poaching, robbery and even murder were not uncommon in rural England, but Stephen and his friends had a different aim. They had sworn to rescue Edward.

Though Stephen had taken part in the Baron's Revolt and had been obliged to go into exile, he was one of those who had rebelled not against Edward but against his advisers, the Despensers. Returning with Isabel's army, his sympathies were now with the ex-king. Stephen's significance lies in the fact that he was the brother of Robert Dunhead, Edward's faithful chaplain who was sharing his captivity at Kenilworth. A plan was being prepared.

Roger Mortimer, a mere baron from the Welsh Marches, could never forget that Henry of Lancaster's wealth and royal descent made him the natural leader of any future movement to overthrow him. He had good reason to fear this. Some barons already resented the almost royal manner that he had begun to assume. Others, with the bishops, were affronted by his unconcealed adulterous relationship with Isabel. Very many less important men like Stephen Dunhead and his friends felt pity for the fallen king in his humiliation. Resistance to royal misgovernment could be justified; the dethronement and imprisonment of the anointed head of the English nation was an altogether different matter.

At the same time the Scots, always ready to take advantage of any confusion or weakness of government in England, again began raiding the north, driving off cattle, seizing grain and looting and burning houses. The barons, and especially those whose lands were being plundered, demanded that something be done to teach the raiders respect for the northern borders. Edward I had set a standard in this action. His son had failed to live up to it; this had contributed to his downfall.

Roger Mortimer could not afford to ignore the challenge. He had to be successful in war if his leadership was to be accepted, but he was in a difficult position. If he led an army against the Scots, dare he leave Edward behind in Kenilworth Castle, from which he might be rescued? He did not trust Henry of Lancaster, suspecting that the earl might already be in communication with Dunhead and others with the same aim.

After anxious consultation with the queen, Mortimer decided that a more secure prison must be found. It may well be that they had already begun to plan Edward's death, as the only way to remove a danger likely to grow more menacing as time passed.

There was an obvious candidate for the post of gaoler of the dethroned king. As we have seen, Mortimer's son-in-law, Thomas Lord Berkeley, had every reason to hate Edward. He had been shut up for four and a half years, separated from his young wife, herself detained for all this time. His father had died miserably as a prisoner in Wallingford. His castle had been looted and his manors plundered by the Despensers. The man of thirty-four who was released from prison by Mortimer's successful coup must have been much changed from the young knight who had, with his father, led the Berkeley troop in the attack on Newport and the Despenser lands in 1321. Used to a life of continuous activity, constantly engaged in war, the tournament and the chase, he had been condemned to years of inaction. Dominated no doubt by his formidable father-in-law Thomas would be a dependable custodian of the royal prisoner.

Nor could Mortimer have found a more suitable prison than Berkeley. Although in its site and style of fortification it did not compare with the great strongholds of the kingdom, it was compact and capable of being held by Berkeley knights and men-at-arms until help could be sent. It was remote from London and the estates of the great earls and their private armies of retainers. Thomas himself was lord of all the manors within many miles of his castle. Between Gloucester and Bristol almost every landholding knight was a Berkeley, or linked by marriage to the Berkeley's or a traditional ally of the family.

Mortimer made his first move early in March. Thomas and one of his knights, Sir William de Wauton who had taken part in the attempted rescue of Maurice de Berkeley from Wallingford Castle, were appointed custodians of the peace for Gloucestershire. This placed the whole county under Thomas's supervision and control, authorising him to take any measure he thought necessary for the security of Berkeley.

Early in April Thomas appeared at Kenilworth at the head of the strongest escort that Berkeley could muster. Edward was delivered to him by indenture, like any piece of property. With Thomas came his brother-in-law, Sir John Maltravers, who after his four years in exile was certainly no friend of the ex-king. Closely guarded by men who had once fought under his command at Bannockburn, Edward began his journey to the castle where he was to meet his cruel death.

That journey was quickly made. Gloucester was reached in two days, on the eve of Palm Sunday. The party lodged in the Augustinian Priory of Llanthony St. Mary, just outside the city wall. It was thought best to avoid the great Abbey of St. Peter where Edward had so often been entertained on state visits to the West and only a few weeks before as a fugitive. Mass on that Palm Sunday morning must have been a sad and embarrassing occasion for the canons.

No time was lost at Llanthony. If the news of the presence of the former king should reach the citizens of Gloucester there was a danger that some attempt at rescue would be made. Though it was a Sunday the journey was continued at once. Berkeley was reached that evening and Edward was lodged in his prison, probably the narrow chamber in the forebuilding at the foot of the keep. Here his outlook was limited to a small courtyard, in contrast to the wide grass-covered bailey of Kenilworth.

A few of Edward's personal attendants came with him to Berkeley; Pancio di Cotrone, his Italian physician, Robert Dunhead, his confessor and some servants. Mortimer and Isabel, in the name of the young king, made Thomas a handsome allowance of five pounds a day, much greater than that received by Henry of Lancaster, for the maintenance of the 'household of the Lord Edward, sometime king of England, our father'. This must have been intended to cover the cost of a strengthened guard. Records long preserved at Berkeley show generous provision of wine, capons, pigeons, kids, eggs and cheese. They ate well at the castle that summer. The chronicler John Capgrave says that Isabel sent her husband 'pleasant gifts and clothes ful precious' but pretended that the magnates would not allow her to visit him. But Capgrave wrote more than a hundred years after the event and one suspects that he was just embroidering his story of Isabel's hatred of her husband.

Now that Edward was at Berkeley, Mortimer seems not to have feared that any attempt at rescue would be made. Within a few days of his return, Thomas received a summons to appear at Newcastle-upon-Tyne by Ascension Day with his usual contingent of knights and their attendant men-at-arms. He was also instructed to bring with him all the weapons and armour kept in the royal castle of Bristol, commandeering the wagons necessary for their transport. With a dozen of his great war horses from the

Gateway of the Priory of Llanthony St. Mary, Gloucester.

stables at Wotton-under-Edge the convoy set out on the long march
northwards along roads familiar enough to Thomas and Sir John
Maltravers though it was eight years since they had last answered the call to
service against the Scots. Sir William Wauton was left in charge of the
castle and its prisoner.

Mortimer's campaign was a failure. The Scots, who had been plundering
the northern counties much as they pleased, avoided the conventional battle
that the English barons wanted in order to wipe out the memory of
Bannockburn. Pursuing their usual guerilla tactics they succeeded in
making Mortimer look foolish. One night, in a famous escapade, James
Douglas crept into the heart of the English camp, cut the guy ropes of the
young king's pavilion and disappeared unharmed in the confusion. When at
last Mortimer seemed to have brought about a confrontation at Stanhope
Park, near York, the Scots outwitted him and slipped away home without
loss.

Though he had not suffered a disastrous defeat, Mortimer's attempt to
deal with the Scottish problem had ended in frustration and humbled pride.
More seriously, his reputation as an able and successful soldier had been
damaged. Military prowess was the yardstick by which the barons judged
their leaders; it was in this quality that Edward II had been found
wanting.

In this atmosphere of gloom and disappointment, alarming news came
from Berkeley. Armed men had forced their way into the castle, seized the
ex-king and carried him off. It is not difficult to imagine the consternation at
York: the anger of Mortimer, the dismay of his closest associates and the
mutterings of those barons who scented a dramatic change of fortunes. But,
as always, Mortimer acted with decision. Thomas and Sir John, 'charged
with the special business of the King' were instantly sent in pursuit. The
very large sum of two hundred pounds was provided for their expenses; an
indication of the size and extent of the search that was to be made.

For this purpose Thomas and Maltravers were made by commission
under the Great Seal 'principal and chief' keepers of the peace for a wide
area in the west and south-west, extending from Gloucester down to Dorset
and from Hereford across to Berkshire. John Smyth, who saw the old writ,
says that they were also given authority to punish offenders by death, that is,
to act also as royal justices. It was unprecedented for such power to be
placed in the hands of two men, one a baron not of the first importance, the
other a mere knight. A clear case of keeping the business in the family;

Mortimer trusted them implicitly. He could be much less certain of the earls.

The war horses and the heavy armour were left behind at York, to be brought home later by the Berkeley retainers. Thomas and his party set off on a punishing ride of more than two hundred miles, along roads thick with summer dust when the sun shone, on rainy days deep in mud. Sometimes their route took them through the territories of barons and knights whose loyalty to Isabel was by no means assured if the news of Edward's escape should become known. No doubt Thomas carried with him writs that ensured a constant supply of fresh horses along the way, but even so it is not likely that Berkeley was reached in much less than a week. The commission under the Great Seal was given on 1st July and Thomas was discharged from his military service at York two days later. Smyth says that Thomas was back home on 4th July, but this must be an error. Thirty miles a day was then reckoned to be very fast going and twenty was more usual. Allowing for the time it had taken for the news to reach York, the rescue party must have had at least a fortnight's start.

What exactly happened at Berkeley in the absence of Thomas? The rescue of the dethroned king is a mysterious episode. Only with difficulty can the story be pieced together, since the government did everything possible to keep the affair secret. But with the little documentary evidence that has survived and a study of Berkeley Castle and its neighbourhood we can try to reconstruct the sequence of events with a fair degree of probability.

The rescue was the work of Stephen Dunhead and his band. A third brother, Thomas Dunhead, had been sent to Avignon just before Edward's fall to find out whether the Pope would be cooperative enough the grant the king a divorce from Queen Isabel. A hopeless mission, given that Pope John XXII was a Frenchman, exiled from Rome, living in a tiny county almost surrounded by the territory of Isabel's brother, Charles IV.

Thomas returned to find his master in prison. He was a Dominican, a preaching friar and, like his brother, a man of courage. He at once joined Stephen on Dunsmore where he found a motley but formidable band of outlaws. There were knights who had been in Edward's service. others had been members of the king's bodyguard. In the Friar Tuck tradition several were fighting priests, some from Gloucestershire. William, canon of Llanthony, must have seen Edward there on Palm Sunday and made up his mind at once as to where his duty lay. A monk from Hailes Abbey and the vicar of Huntley, near Gloucester, had come with him. A handful of turbulent friars, eager to join in any violent action, and equally ready to give absolution to any who shared in it. A gang like this attracted not only men who were there out of loyalty to Edward but rough and boisterous characters drawn by the prospect of enjoyable mayhem.

For some weeks they had been roaring around the Midlands, making trouble and recruiting the disaffected. As soon as Edward had been brought to Berkeley they came to Gloucestershire, stirring up a riot in Cirencester that led Mortimer to issue a writ for their arrest. This accused Stephen Dunhead of avoiding service against the Scots but carefully avoided any mention of the real purpose of his activities. He and his men promptly disappeared, turning up a few weeks later in Cheshire where their lawless behaviour led to charges of homicide before they returned to shelter in their base on Dunsmore.

Thomas's absence in Yorkshire provided them with their opportunity. Some time in mid-June they made their way to Berkeley in ones and twos, the priests among them possibly in the guise of pilgrims. Their journey took them over the sparsely populated uplands of the Cotswolds. Between the western edge of these 'high, wild ways' and the castle of Berkeley lay the great oak forest of Michaelwood, in the recesses of which such a band of men could secretely gather. Though it might have been expected that news of the arrival of a large body of strangers would have been given to the constable of the castle by Berkeley retainers in the country around, apparently this did not happen.

The Dunheads faced a seemingly impossible task. They had somehow to obtain entrance through the gatehouse that led into the outer bailey, when they would find themselves facing an even stronger gatehouse and the walls of the massive Norman keep. Only through this second gate could they gain access to the inner courtyard. Then they could only get into the keep by climbing a narrow outer staircase at the head of which was a door leading into the first floor, where Edward was held prisoner. The stair was so commanded from the forebuilding that two or three determined men could hold it against many times their number. Inside the keep the passages were so narrow and the rooms so small that attackers could easily be struck down.

We shall never know whether the Dunheads gained entry in the daytime or during the night, or how it was done. In the absence of Thomas and Sir John Maltravers the castle garrison must have been very lax to have

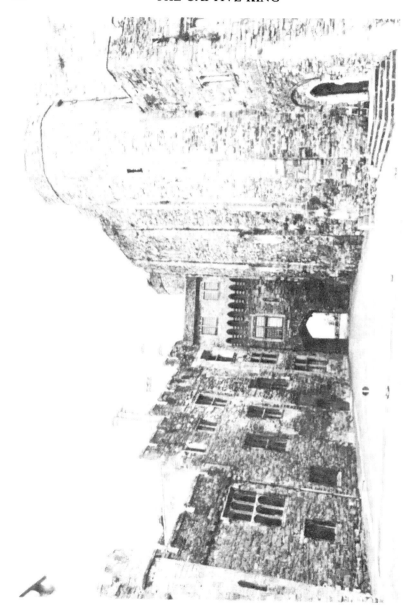

Berkeley Castle. Courtyard and Keep, with Forebuilding.

allowed themselves to be surprised. However that may be, Sir William
Wauton was never blamed for the escape. Perhaps he was at his nearby
manor of Cromhall that night. At all events he continued in the service of
Lord Thomas until the end of his life.

It is likely that the raiding party assembled during the night in the thickets
of Berkeley Heath, which then reached almost to the castle walls. Entry
may have been effected in the morning, either by stratagem or connivance.
Did Thomas Dunhead appear at the gatehouse and ask to see his brother?
Perhaps a few of the monks or friars, who were certainly pretty though
customers, slipped in with him, overpowered the guard and admitted a
sufficient number of their accomplices to hold off the alerted garrison whilst
Edward was brought out of the keep.

All this could not have been done without the help of some of the guards
immediately around the ex-king. Perhaps Robert Dunhead had been able to
win over some members of the garrison and pass out information to his
brothers. How else could the rescuers have known exactly where Edward
was imprisoned? The raid must have been carried out quickly. One cannot
believe that the whole castle was taken over whilst a lengthy search was
made. Even in the absence of Lord Thomas and his troop there were some
two hundred people living within the walls.

Whatever their method, the Dunheads succeeded in getting Edward out
of the castle and away into Michaelwood, through which they were able to
pass into Kingswood Chase, a vast hunting ground of oak woods, bramble,
furze and bracken, stretching twenty miles southward to the banks of the
Avon between Bristol and Bath. Their flight thus covered, they were able to
cross into Somerset by the ancient bridge at Keynsham. Were they perhaps
sheltered for a night or two in the Augustinian abbey there? Across the
deserted wastes of Mendip and through the forest of Selwood the
triumphant band headed for the Dorset coast with the intention of getting
the ex-king out of the country. Edward himself must have been filled with
renewed hope, though he would have been faced with another hazardous
journey through France, where he could expect no friendly reception from
Isabel's family.

Immediately after the rescue Dr. John Walwayn, a high government
official, was sent down to Berkeley to conduct an investigation. It is from a
brief report by him that we know about the 'armed force that came to the
castle of Berkeley and ravished the father of our Lord the King out of our
guard and feloniously robbed the said castle against the King's peace'.

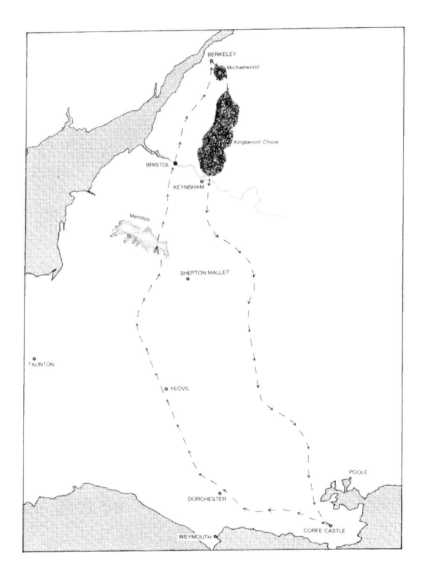

Edward II's escape, recapture and return to Berkeley.

Walwayn clearly realised that there were difficulties about bringing a charge against the raiders since, in the eyes of the law, Edward could not be a prisoner. He had never been tried or convicted. He had left Berkeley willingly; it was his arrest and continued detention that were illegal.

The Dunheads and Edward must have been well on their way when Berkeley and Maltravers were sent in pursuit. Evidently they had not been caught at the end of July, when Walwayn made his report. He had identified the raiders and on 1st August a writ was sent to Thomas ordering him to arrest the two Dunheads and a number of others who were named. The hue and cry was intensified; the party was eventually cornered somewhere near Corfe Castle. Perhaps it had been a mistake to head for Dorset, where the Maltravers family were important landowners and Sir John himself governor of the castle. It may be that relatives and retainers prevented the fugitives from getting a ship. A swiftly riding horseman could perhaps have brought news of the escape in time to enable them to alert the ports and hold off the Dunheads until Lord Thomas and his men arrived. It is this episode that explains the appearance of Corfe Castle in some of the chronicles as the place of Edward's imprisonment and murder. He must have lodged there for a short time after his recapture.

Thomas Dunhead was taken with him. According to one account he was brought before Isabel before being sent to Pontefract Castle, where he was tortured, murdered and thrown down a disused well. The brave Stephen Dunhead escaped, was captured in London a few months later, got away a second time and was never caught by Mortimer's men. When arrested in London he was again charged with refusing to serve against the Scots and with plundering Berkeley Castle, but no mention was made of the rescue of Edward. Two other members of his band were caught near Edward's old manor house at King's Langley and were imprisoned in Newgate, but nothing is known of their fate. Mortimer and Isabel drew over the whole affair a curtain of silence which was never lifted by Edward III.

While the fugitives were being hunted down, Edward was brought back to Berkeley by Maltravers and Sir Thomas Gournay, a member of another branch of the Berkeley family. He was to play a sinister part in the final act of the tragedy. It was on this journey that the indignities were heaped upon the fallen king, as narrated by Geoffrey Baker in his chronicle. 'They would crown him with a crown of hay and shave his head and beard by the roadside with ditchwater, to make a zany of him'. Baker says that he had this part of the story from one William Bishop, one of the escort. Some historians have dismissed this as another picturesque addition, because Bishop cannot be identified. Hardly a sufficient reason; it is not possible to identify any of the squires and men-at-arms who made up the party. Indeed the story has the mark of probability about it. The chronicler John Stow, writing in Elizabethan times, said that this was done to disguise the prisoner. He and his guards were passing through country where sympathy might easily be aroused. His long fair hair and handsome curled beard would quickly lead to recognition and another attempt to release him. The shaving and haircutting would be an obvious precaution against this.

The party returned through Bristol, staying in the castle there for a few days. It was said that when rumours of Edward's presence reached the townspeople some of them began to prepare for his rescue and the return to Berkeley had to be hurriedly completed.

After this Edward was kept in much stricter custody and treated as a common prisoner, though we have no very reliable information about this. He was moved into a cell in the keep itself, which must have been gloomy and unpleasant enough. But the oft-repeated tale that, in an attempt to destroy his health, he was kept in a chamber above a pit filled by his gaolers with rotting carcases is a later invention. There were more effective ways of bringing this about, had they wished to do so.

Gournay remained at Berkeley. He and Maltravers acted as gaolers, alternating daily as supervisors of the prisoner. However, the story that Lord Thomas was ordered to hand Edward over to them and relieved of all responsibility for him has no evidence to support it. It was probably circulated after the fall of Mortimer in an attempt to exonerate Thomas from blame. When he was eventually arraigned before Parliament the indictment made it clear that Edward had remained in his custody.

The dethroned king was now at the mercy of three men who had every reason to bear him a good deal of ill will. Thomas and Maltravers had suffered at the hands of Edward and the Despensers, and so had Sir Thomas Gournay. He was descended from a younger son of Robert, the first Fitzharding Lord of Berkeley. The Gournays had inherited very large estates in Yorkshire and the West Country, including Beverstone Castle on the Cotswolds just above Berkeley. Their wealth was probably greater than that of the senior line.

In due course the Gournay lands in Gloucestershire passed by marriage to one John ap Adam. He died when his son was still a child; the profitable wardship of his estate given to the younger Despenser, ever on the lookout to increase his personal fortune. Wardships were much sought after. The fortunate recipient, after making suitable provision for the widow and children, could do much as he pleased with the rest of the income, so long as he fulfilled his military obligations to the Crown. Sir Thomas Gournay, whose own lands were in Somerset, was cousin to the boy heir. He resented being passed over for the wardship. When the barons rose in revolt in 1321 he joined them in the raids on the Despenser manors. When he went on to Boroughbridge he was outlawed and his lands seized. The next few years he spent in exile. He was not well disposed to the ex-king.

After the return to Berkeley the castle was strongly guarded and every precaution taken against another rescue attempt. It was at this time that Thomas succeeded in arresting some of the Despenser officials who had despoiled his castle and manors while he was imprisoned at Pevensey. They were shut up in the castle but there is no record of their trial or release. But in the 1920s when extensive restoration was being undertaken by the last Earl of Berkeley six skeletons were found under a staircase near the keep. They may or may not have been those of Despenser's men. They could equally well be those of Berkeley "traitors" who had connived at Edward's escape, or men who knew too much, or some of the Dunhead band. These bones suggest that the murder of the ex-king was not the only deed of darkness done by ruthless men.

The tragedy now moved rapidly towards its dreadful climax. Early in September there was much unrest in North Wales, where Mortimer was no more loved than any of the Marcher lords whose ancestors had deprived the Welsh of their tribal lands. Sir Griffyth Lloyd, the loyal henchman whose capture of Chirk Castle had led to the Mortimer surrender in 1321 did not attend the coronation of the young king and ignored a summons to Parliament. He now appeared in the mountains under the nom de guerre of Sir Rhys ap Gryffydd as the leader of a rebel force. Edward had always been quite popular in North Wales; there was never any lack of young Welshmen ready for adventure. After the failure in Yorkshire and winter approaching, Mortimer was in no position to lead an expedition against him. Lloyd was secure in the mountains and, it is said, approached some English barons with proposals for an attack on Berkeley. William of Shalford, Mortimer's deputy as Justiciar of Wales, was much alarmed by reports of Lloyd's activities. He wrote to Mortimer, warning him of the danger.

Mortimer had been growing increasingly uneasy about the situation. Probably he and Isabel, after the Dunheads' attempt had so narrowly failed, had made up their minds that only Edward's death would remove the continuing threat to their security. More barons were showing signs of dissatisfaction with the regime. Sooner or later, if Edward lived, another effort would be made to get him out and perhaps to restore him to the throne. Isabel had gone too far to draw back. Her love for Mortimer, her lust for wealth and power, all drove her to the fatal conclusion. Edward must die. Mortimer again acted with decision.

From the Marches a number of sinister characters converged on Berkeley. One William of Ocle was the man recruited to carry out the murder.

Ocle brought with him for Thomas's information Shalford's letter which allegedly contained the notorious phrase 'Edwardum occidere timere bonum est', said to have been composed by Adam Orleton, Bishop of Hereford, which could mean either 'Fear not to kill the king, 'tis good he die', or 'Kill not the king, 'tis good to fear the worst', according to the placing of a stop. But Orleton had been in France since the beginning of April and could not have been involved in the plot. With Ocle came Sir Simon de Barford, or Bereford, who was afterwards named as taking part in the actual murder. There also appeared at the castle a female embalmer, whose arrival was indeed ominous.

CHAPTER SIX

"THEY SHORTENED HIS LIFE"

*'The King must die, or Mortimer
goes down, The Commons now begin to pity him."*
MARLOWE: EDWARD II

So completely was Edward kept in isolation that we know nothing of his thoughts, his words, his relations with his gaolers or his physical condition after so many months of confinement. Mentally he may have been in a poor state, but his powerful constitution is not likely to have been much affected. One would give much to know what was said and done at Berkeley after the arrival of William of Ocle, but what followed is hidden in deepest shadow. "What secret intelligence passed between father-in-law and son", wrote John Smyth in 1628, "I will not further conjecture". His long and careful examination of the Berkeley archives evidently revealed no document that threw any light upon the crime. Had he found one, Smyth was too honest to have suppressed it.

We are therefore dependent upon the chroniclers for the story of the dethroned king's last days. Usually monks or canons, these medieval annalists often wrote long after the events they describe. They compiled their records for their own monastery or cathedral libraries and the laboriously written copies over the next fifty or one hundred years slowly found their way into other enclosed communities and, perhaps, to Oxford and Cambridge. The chronicle was not, therefore, 'published' in the modern sense and subjected to the criticism of an army of scholars or of men who had played a part in the making of history. And like authors of today, the chroniclers were often biased by jealousies, prejudices and allegiances. Kings and barons who had been generous to the Church tended to get a good press; those who had been in conflict with it had their failings emphasised or exaggerated.

The *St. Paul's Annales,* judged to have been written by one of the canons within a few years of these events, record the death of Edward without explanation or comment. Soon afterwards another writer hints that he had not died a natural death. Not until some thirty years later did Ralph Higden, canon of St. Werberg's in Chester, author of a sort of universal history of the world called *Polychronicon,* written in Latin, describe what happened. Passing fairly rapidly from Biblical times to the night of 21st September 1327 at Berkeley, he says that ruffians hired by Mortimer burst into Edward's cell, overpowered him and murdered him by thrusting a red hot spit into his bowels through a horn inserted in the rectum, a hideous method which left no visible trace of the means employed.

We do not know the source of Higden's account of the murder. He may have been repeating hearsay, he may have had first-hand information or he may simply have made up a horror story to liven up his manuscript. Whatever the truth, this is the version that was adopted by later chroniclers like the Elizabethan John Stow from whom Christopher Marlowe got the details for the horrific death scene in his play *Edward the Second.*

One would think that suffocation alone would have been sufficiently effective; indeed this must also have been used, if Higden's story is true, to stifle the victim's cries of agony, since death would be far from instantaneous.

Edward was a well-built, powerful man so it is likely that there were five or six in the murder party. Sir Thomas Gournay, Sir Simon de Barford and Sir John Maltravers were the men in charge of the assassination; William of Ocle and other 'hired Ruffians' probably carried out the dreadful crime. Thomas Berkeley can hardly have been unaware of what was planned and accomplished.

Exactly what happened has never been known. No evidence has ever been found to corroborate Higden's account but one single fact suggest that it may have been true. The *Polychronicon* was translated into English between 1379 and 1387 by John of Trevisa, the Oxford scholar who became vicar of Berkeley and chaplain of Thomas (IV) Lord Berkeley, grandson of Thomas (III) who was Edward's gaoler. *Trevisa did not suppress or alter the passage dealing with the murder. From this one may perhaps conclude that the details were common knowledge at Berkeley.

---

*John Smyth (Lives of the Berkeleys), Vol. 1, pp 11 & 344, made one of his rare mistakes in his account of Trevisa. He says that the translation was made at the request of Thomas III. This is improbable as Trevisa was then a youth of about seventeen who had not yet taken his degree at Oxford where he became a fellow of Exeter college in 1362. He came to Berkeley in 1379 and in his introduction to the translation says that he completed it in 1387. In a marginal note to his own manuscript Smyth says that he 'corrected' the date to 1357; he made other alterations to the introduction to support the change.

When Trevisa was working on his translation, less than fifty years after the murder, there would certainly have been some old retainers at the castle who had been boys or young men at the time and would know well enough what had happened. Evidently Thomas IV, a soldier and politician who played a part in the deposition, again followed by murder, of Edward's great-grandson, Richard II, was not sensitive about the family past. Indeed he had no need to be, since Thomas III was eventually acquitted of complicity.

The only comment on Edward's death to come directly from Berkeley was recorded by Jean Froissart, the most famous of all medieval chroniclers. He visited Berkeley in 1366.

'After the king had arrived at Berkeley he did not live long. And how could he have lived long when things were as I tell you? In order to confirm my chronicle I inquired about the king, asking what had become of him. An old squire told me that in the same year that he was taken there he died, for they shortened his life for him. So ended that king of England and we shall speak no more of him'.

It is difficult to believe that the tireless questioner and recorder of contemperary history did not hear a good deal more than this. He came to Berkeley only five years after the death of Lord Thomas (III) so the old squire had quite possibly been present in the castle on that September night. He must have known who 'they' were and how Edward's life was 'shortened'. Froissart seems to end on a note of caution, as though it were best not to say too much.

Froissart did not lead a cloistered life. At this time he was a member of the household of Philippa of Hainault, Edward III's queen and during his seven years at court he must have heard the events of 1327 discussed. His position may have made him wary. Unlike the monkish chroniclers he was in the habit of reading aloud his stories to barons and knights who were politically active and it would perhaps have been imprudent to say too much on such a dangerous subject. So Jean Froissart, who might have given us something near the whole truth, rode away from Berkeley 'after three pleasant days in the castle and in amusements in the neighbourhood' and chose to remember only that 'they shortened his life for him'.

On the morrow of the murder Lord Thomas wrote a letter informing Isabel and Mortimer of Edward's death. This was sent to Nottingham by the hand of Sir Thomas Gournay, for which service the knight received thirty-one shillings to cover the cost of his ride. Some days later he returned, with instructions that the news should be kept secret until All Saints' Day, and this was done.

Meanwhile, for the rest of September and the whole of October the body lay in the little chapel of St. John in the keep, where daily oblations were offered for the repose of Edward's soul. Was Lord Thomas present on any of these occasions? Did he, during hose days, make his confessions to his caplain there? John Smyth's keen eye detected that between the murder and the funeral Thomas spent his days in 'hawking, hunting and other sports of the field'. It was of course necessary to preserve an appearance of normality during these weeks, but he and his associates must have been hard men to continue in this say of life whilst the body of the victim was still in his castle.

When at last the announcement of the death was made, according to a chronicler who wrote long afterwards, burgesses from Bristol and Gloucester and local knights were admitted to view the body. If this was so, they must have realised that the king had been dead for some time. The chronicler adds that the body showed no mark of violence, but the features were contorted in agony.

The government assumed responsibility for the funeral arrangements. Isabel sent a royal clerk, Hugh de Glanville, to take charge. The embalmer had carried out her gruesome task and a silver cup valued at thirty-seven shillings and eightpence was provided for Edward's heart which, incredibly, was sent to Isabel. One wonders what happened to it. It was decided that the funeral should take place in the abbey of St. Peter, in the royal city of Gloucester. The choice was Isabel's, as the most suitable and convenient place. There is no foundation for the assertion of a later abbot of St. Peter's that the abbots of Malmesbury, Kingswood and St. Augustine's at Bristol all refused to receive the body for fear of the queen's displeasure, though the story was repeated by John Smyth and is still told locally.

The long delay was necessary firstly to enable Mortimer to prepare for possible hostile reaction to the news, and more prosaically to the fact that the government department from which supplies had to be drawn for a state funeral was still with the army in Yorkshire.

Not until early November did Edward II, of the Plantagenet line of the kings of England, begin his last journey from Berkeley to Gloucester. It was in all respects a contrast to the funeral procession of his father, whose body twenty years before had been brought from Carlisle to Westminster with all the ceremony due to a dead king. At every cathedral and monastery of

Edward II. Detail of effigy in Gloucester Cathedral.

importance that cortege had rested overnight, so that masses might be sung. There was no regal dignity about the second Edward's progress to his tomb. A handful of men-at-arms, black pennoned lances at rest, helmets hanging from their saddles, led the way. An aged abbot mounted on his palfrey was followed by black-robed monks, walking two and two. Lumbering behind them came a huge broad-wheeled chariot covered by a black pall of rough canvas, drawn by six black horses. A silent group of armed knights in black surcoats followed, not too closely, and more men-at-arms brought up the rear.

Early that morning Edward's body had been brought out through the castle gatehouse into the market place of the town, watched by a crowd of burgesses and bondsmen, bareheaded before their late king and, more to the point, before their Lord Thomas, who rode out flanked by his kinsmen and escorted by his guard. For a month and two weeks the people of Berkeley had lived in the shadow of the Norman keep and its dreadful secret; since the night, so it is said, when agonized cries awakened some of them from early sleep. Many days later the death of the king had been announced and messengers began to come and go between Berkeley and the court. There were whisperings as those who served in the castle came into the town on business and into the alehouses—but only between those who could trust each other, for here the Lord of Berkeley had power of life and death, as they well knew.

Now in this late autumn morning there was only a silence, broken by the solemn chanting of the monks and the creaking of the chariot wheels. Abbot Thokey of St. Peter's had come in person with all those monks who were able to make the journey, bringing with him his own chariot, adorned with the arms of the abbey. From the castle the procession descended the hill, crossed the bridge over the Doverle brook and passed over Berkeley Heath to the long straight road built by the Romans more than a thousand years before, now rutted and difficult. The cortege progressed slowly along it. From time to time the chariot had to be manhandled over rough places and the coffin rocked dangerously.

The leaves were thinning in the topmost branches of the elm trees, where the rooks perched beside their empty nests. Overhead flew the skeins of wild geese on their way to the winter feeding grounds on the Severn shore. The cattle of the marshlands stood to watch; in the villages silent little groups of men and women had gathered. For much of the way the funeral procession moved through the lands of the Honour of Berkeley. At every mile it halted and the chanting of the monks was heard again. The knights and men-at-arms dismounted, eased the harness of their horses and whispered to each other. Later, at each of these stopping places the people of Gloucestershire planted an oak tree. For many hundreds of years these marked the melancholy route. Husbandmen told the story to their children who in turn repeated it; their descendents in the cottages of the Berkeley Vale were still doing so early in this century.

When dusk fell the body rested in a village church, watched throughout the night by the monks while the men-at-arms lay uncomfortably on the floor. Lord Thomas and his knights slept, perhaps more easily, in the hall of a neighbouring manor house. Next day the journey was completed; the cortege arrived at the south gate of Gloucester. Here waited the mayor and burgesses, the canons of Llanthony and the monks of St. Oswald's, the Dominican and Franciscan friars and the clergy of the parish churches.

From the gate the cortege passed through the narrow streets to one of those city churches, where the coffin was to lie for some weeks while preparations were made for the burial in the abbey. Thomas's responsibilities were at an end. The body of the murdered king had been safely delivered. Thomas had been well paid for his trouble. Twelve hundred pounds in all had found their way from the Exchequer to Berkeley. When all the expenses of the past six months had been met a very satisfactory profit was left. After all, the oblations for Edward's soul cost no more than twenty-one pence.

Throughout November and the greater part of December the body awaited burial. Isabel, having disposed of her husband, was determined that there should be a funeral ceremony of truly royal splendour. More than seven hundred pounds was made available for the arrangements, now placed under the supervision of Sir John Dancy. The see of Worcester, in which Gloucester lay, being vacant, the Bishop of Llandaff was instructed to come to Gloucester and remain in readiness. He was John Eaglescliff, a friar of Edward's favourite Dominican order. He had to wait for nearly two months, but his retaining fee of thirteen shillings and fourpence a day doubtless made his stay endurable. Several knights, two royal chaplains and three sergeants-at-arms were also in constant attendance, waiting for the arrival from London of Andrew, the King's candlemaker, who brought the hearse. He and his assistants provided light in the dim recesses of the Norman nave and choir.

On 21st December the funeral procession again moved through the city

streets on its way to St. Peter's. Stout barriers of oak from the Forest of
Dean had been erected to hold back the crowds that gathered to watch the
long column of barons and knights, all of whom had been provided with new
robes at the royal expense.

It is not easy to picture the immense hearse on which the coffin was
carried. The accounts for the cost of its construction have survived. It was
surmounted by effigies of the four evangelists and four great golden lions
made by John Eastwick, the King's Painter. Below were eight angels
holding gold censers and on the sides were the royal arms of England.
Golden leopards were emblazoned on the harness of the horses; more than
eight hundred gold leaves were used to cover the hearse.

Immediately behind it rode knights carrying royal standards and a forest
of pennants. In the crowded abbey waited Queen Isabel, the young Edward
III and the impassive Mortimer who had come to see the man he most hated
and had most wronged committed to the grave. What Isabel and her son felt
as they listened to the noble Gregorian chant of the funeral mass is not
known to us. Nor has anything been recorded of the feelings of Henry of
Lancaster and the other great magnates who were perhaps beginning to
realise that they had made Roger Mortimer the real master of the kingdom.
Had Thomas and his father-in-law any foreboding of the consequences of
their criminal conspiracy? Or were they satisfied that they had now made
themselves secure from any reversal of fortune? We may be sure that there
were plenty of guilty and uneasy minds in that great gathering of the nobility
of England.

Whatever the barons were thinking, the common people had already
made up their minds. As soon as Edward's body was laid to rest and the
wooden image with its gilt crown placed above it, the pilgrims began to
come with their offerings to the tomb of one whom they called saint and
martyr. How should this have been, if the truth about Edward's death had
not been known in Gloucestershire? And if ordinary folk knew or suspected
the truth, could all the magnates have been ignorant of the deed of Lord
Thomas and his kinsmen?

The wooden figure of the ex-king was soon replaced by the recumbent
alabaster effigy which we see today, one of the earliest and finest of tomb
sculptures in this white translucent stone, much used in the fourteenth
century for images of the great and famous. Edward's head rests on a pillow
supported by two angels; his feet rest upon a lion. The sceptre he holds in his
left hand has now, somewhat fitly, been broken and the cross has gone from

the top of the orb held in his right. His body is draped in a gracefully flowing robe, typical of the exquisite sculptors' work of the time.

Edward is portrayed as a handsome, robust man in early middle age, the face framed in delicately carved wavy hair and beard. Whether the sculptor achieved a real likeness we cannot know, but since the effigy was in place a few years after Edward's death he may well have been acquainted with the king's appearance or have worked from a portrait. The sensual features do not lack dignity and refinement and agree with what we know of Edward's character and looks. It is certainly the most remarkable of all the effigies of English medieval kings.

The tomb itself matches the figure in beauty. Above the recumbent form rise the fretted spires and slender supporting columns of a translucent double canopy most skilfully carved in Cotswold stone of the finest grain. The tomb chest below is of Purbeck marble, with arched recesses that once sheltered more than two dozen little mourning figures. Effigy and tomb together are a memorable example of medieval art in full flower.

There is a story that Edward, on a visit to the abbey, once admired the portraits of his predecessors painted on the refectory wall and asked if his own would one day be added. Abbot Thokey is said to have replied that he hoped to give his king an even worthier memorial. There is a flavour of hindsight about the anecdote but, true or not, Edward is more magnificently commemorated than any.

This is the shrine to which pilgrims flocked in their thousands. Many were humble people but among them several times came King Edward III, his queen Phillipa, their son the Black Prince and queen Joan of Scotland. It has been said that Edward encouraged the cult of his father to rival that of Thomas of Lancaster, but the unofficial canonisation of the murdered king was the spontaneous tribute of ordinary men. No royal patronage was needed.

The lavish gifts of the royal family on the offerings of the pilgrims brought great wealth to St. Peter's. Abbot Thokey died within a year of the funeral and was succeeded by Abbot Wigmore whose name suggests that he may have been a protege of Mortimer. Almost at once he began the transformation of the great monastic chapel. The walls of the presbytery and the transepts were raised and enormous windows inserted to let in the sunlight. The walls were heightened and the Norman arcades covered by the tall Perpendicular columns that we see today. The eastern apse disappeared to be replaced by the largest window of painted glass in England.

Tomb of Edward II in Gloucester Cathedral.

The morning light that falls on Edward's tomb illuminates in its glass the emblazoned shields of Thomas Lord Berkeley and his brother Maurice, their close comrade Thomas de Bradestone and of four great earls of the day, Arundel, Warwick, de Bohun and Lancaster. This magnificent window which can be dated to about 1350 is usually said to be a commemoration of the battle of Crecy, though Thomas himself was not present there. Clearly the window has a Berkeley significance; perhaps the glass, and maybe the window itself, was one of the many of Lord Thomas's acts of expiation.

CHAPTER SEVEN

THE ITALIAN PRIEST'S TALE

*"Like many other kings who died mysteriously,
he became the hero of a tale of wonder."*
BISHOP STUBBS: CHRONICLES OF EDWARD I
AND EDWARD II

No sooner had Edward's body been laid in his tomb than the pilgrims began to arrive in Gloucester. The government had not for a moment admitted that there had been a murder; the official line was that the king had died a natural death, though no attempt at an explanation was made. The omission was noticed. Among ordinary folk there was a feeling that something was wrong. Their reaction was to confer upon him an unofficial canonisation without waiting for the Pope to enthrone him among the saints. In medieval times people often honoured the memory of a person of note in this way. Once it had been done, reports of a miracle or two at the tomb were enough to bring in pilgrims from an ever widening field.

On the other hand, there were those who refused to believe that he was dead. For some years there were persistent rumours that he was being held prisoner in some remote place—Corfe Castle was the favoured spot—or that he had escaped to France. But when, after Mortimer's death, the young Edward III began to make inquiries about the circumstances of his father's death and when the lapse of time made it safe for chroniclers to give their version of what had happened at Berkeley, the doubts faded. They did not appear again until five centuries had passed.

Every historian, eminent or humble, dreams that one day, as he reads through some bundle of faded, forgotten letters or slowly deciphers the half-legible characters of a medieval charter, that he will chance upon something that will disprove some long-accepted story, or throw light on some mysterious episode. This rarely happens. Historical problems, like modern murders, are solved by the painstaking putting together of scraps of evidence.

Yet one of those moments of surprised discovery was given to Professor Germain of the University of Montpellier in the South of France. One day in 1877 when he was examining a collection of fourteenth century documents he found a copy of a letter written to Edward III by a priest named Manuele del Fieschi. He was a member of a wealthy Genoese family that produced many distinguished churchmen, including two popes and several cardinals.

After a short account of the events leading to the imprisonment of Edward II, Fieschi tells the young king that he has just heard the confession of an Englishman (who, of course, he does not name) to the effect that his father was not, as is generally believed, murdered at Berkeley. Here, says Fieschi, is the story of what actually happened.

All arrangements had been made for the crime. It was essential that they should be known to as few people as possible, so the task of watching over the prisoner that night was given to a single guard. This man, moved by compassion or perhaps fearing that he himself might afterwards be killed in order to ensure complete secrecy, warned the ex-king that Sir Thomas Gournay and Sir Simon Barford were coming to kill him. He begged Edward to escape, offering him a servants' robe that he had brought. The two then made their way to the outer gate where they found the custodian asleep, killed him and stole out of the castle.

When Gournay and Barford entered the prisoner's cell they were horrified to find that Edward had gone. The body of the gatekeeper provided the way out of a difficult situation. It was his heart that was sent to Isabel and his body that was interred with such ceremony at Gloucester.

Meanwhile Edward and his rescuer made their way to Corfe Castle where the constable gave them shelter. Maltravers, the non-resident governor of Corfe, was kept in ignorance of the ex-king's presence. Edward's stay ended when his half-brother, Edmund, Earl of Kent, was arrested and executed on a charge of telling some of the barons that the ex-king was still alive at Corfe. Edward then crossed to Ireland, living there as a hermit for nine months. Returning to England he made his way to Sandwich and crossed over to Sluys, still wearing his hermit's gown. His travels then took him through Normandy, southwards to Languedoc and so to Avignon.

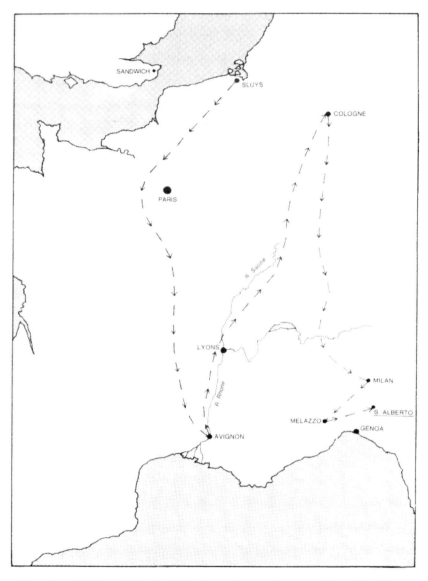

Travels of Edward II after his alleged second escape from Berkeley.

Here the gift of a gold florin to an attendant assured him of an audience with the Pope. John XXII, who must have been considerably astonished by the arrival of this unexpected visitor, entertained him kindly for fifteen days. Then, with a pilgrim's licence provided by the Pope, Edward travelled to Paris and Cologne. The object of the visit to Cologne was to worship at the famous shrine of the Three Kings in the Cathedral. This done, he crossed Germany and passed over the Alps to Milan.

Edward then spent two and a half years in the castle of Melazzo in the Ligurian hills, leaving when war broke out in the district. His final refuge was "the castle of Cecima". For two more years he devoted himself to a life of prayer and penitence in strict seclusion until his death.

On the face of it the story has too many improbabilities; English historians have dismissed it rather summarily and though from time to time it has surfaced in magazine articles, their writers did not examine the letter critically. Some Italian historians have looked at it more carefully. Constantine Nigra first drew the attention of his countrymen to it in 1901 since when several others have written on the subject, notably Professor Anna Benedetti of the University of Palermo in a book published in 1924. On the strength of their researches they are more ready to believe that there is some truth in the story. But there are several objections that need to be considered.

First, is the letter genuine? It was found in the archives of the department of the Herault, in Montpellier in the south of France. Nigra and other scholars who examined it were satisfied that the material on which it was written and the style of the Latin date it to the fourteenth century. The collection of documents, probably from a secretary's office, was put together for a bishop of Maguelonne, near Montpellier, who had been a Papal official at Avignon. The letter bears the seal of a Papal notary, a post that was held by Manuele del Fieschi. It is probable that the letter was written there.

Manuele is a historical personage. We have quite a lot of information about him. Several members of the Fieschi family were international diplomats; some of them had links with the English court. Carlo del Fieschi was actually resident there and was one of the closest advisers of Edward II. Manuele himself held a number of benefices in England. In 1329 he became a canon of the cathedral at York. This was when Isabel and Mortimer were ruling the country; it is possible that Manuele was here on some diplomatic mission and was given the canonry as a souvenir of his visit. Later he added

Castello di Melazzo, Ligurian Apennines.

Tourist Information Office, Alessandria

a canonry of Lincoln and the archdeaconry of Nottingham. Of course he held all these in absentia; canonries and other well-paid benefices were the gilt-edged stock of the Middle Ages; a good portfolio could provide a comfortable income for life. They could even be sold or exchanged.

Is the account of the escape credible? However he gained his information the writer of the letter seems to have some background knowledge of the affair, including the names of two of the men most deeply involved. But the letter makes the escape sound such a simple matter. Would it in fact be possible for two men armed perhaps with no more than a knife or a dagger to get out of the keep in this way? Would there not have been more than one man at the gatehouse? Where were Edward's personal attendants while all this was happening?

It could be that the "gatekeeper" was a guard at the door of the forebuilding or the entrance to the keep and that after killing him the two were able to pass out through the castle gates since it would be assumed by the guards, in the poor light, that they were servants. Though this may not seem very likely it must be remembered that only a few weeks earlier the Dunheads had somehow got the ex-king out of Berkeley in some way that has never been explained. As for his personal attendants, we hear no more of them after Edward's death or disappearance. It is probable that they were kept away from him after the first escape. Certainly they were never called upon by Edward III to give their version of what happened. The evidence of his physician and his confessor would have been highly interesting.

Would it have been possible to pass off the gatekeeper's body as that of Edward whose striking face was, to say the least, unlikely to be duplicated in a castle servant? But although one chronicler says that some notables of Bristol and Gloucestershire were admitted to view the body, this was said long afterwards. The whole affair was so shrouded in secrecy that it is probable that no one outside the small circle of conspirators actually saw the ex-king after his death.

It is noticeable that the letter makes no mention of any pursuit or search. The Dunhead party had been large and presumably most of them had been mounted, yet they were caught. Surely, with all the forces at his disposal, Thomas could have hunted down two poorly armed men trying to get away on foot, without any pre-arranged plan or outside assistance?

The letter would be more convincing if some details of Edward's stay in Ireland had been given, or of his journey across England afterwards. Would it have been possible for him to move about in this way or to take ship from

Wall plaque in the Castello di Melazzo, recording Edward's residence after his alleged escape from Berkeley.

Tourist Information Office, Alessandria

Sandwich without being recognised? It could be that his sufferings had by then changed his fine looks and unmistakable bearing. If he was without his beard and had the cropped head of a priest he could have passed unnoticed in the crowds of pilgrims always on the roads in those days.

Again the letter makes no mention of any person who helped Edward on his travels, until he reached Avignon. Clearly he could not have made those long journeys without the aid of a number of people.

When we turn to the account given of Edward's fortunes after his departure from Avignon we find some details that lend a little credibility to the story. It is said that Pope John provided him with a pilgrim's licence so that he might visit the shrine of the Three Kings. An interesting point, for the relics of the Kings, removed to a place of safety during the rebuilding of the cathedral, had recently been returned to the shrine. Pilgrims were flocking to Cologne in great numbers.

After the pilgrimage, the young king is told, his father sought a permanent sanctuary in northern Italy. The castle of Melazzo, his first refuge, stands on a hilltop above the river Erro, a few miles south of the little modern spa of Acqui Terme, some forty miles north of Genoa. Its grey stone parapets, red-tiled buildings and compact tree-shaded courtyard rise above terraced orchards and vineyards. Today it houses a restaurant. The visitor will find on the wall of a corridor a large marble plaque "correcting the historical error" of the murder of Edward II, recording Professor Germain's discovery and commemorating the ex-king's stay in the castle. This was placed there early this century after Constantine Nigra had identified it as the Melazzo of the story.

It will be asked why Melazzo, of all places should have been chosen as a refuge. It was a possession of the archbishopric of Milan, where Edward first stayed on entering Italy. It is suggested that he was then under the special protection of the Pope, who would have made all the necessary arrangements.

The reason given for his flight from Melazzo accords with history. There was, in fact, an outbreak of feudal warfare in the district at the time of his alleged departure.

Cecima, where he is said to have spent his last years, is a small mountain village built on land rising above the fast-flowing river Staffora, about fifty miles north-east of Genoa. There has never been a castle at Cecima but it is a walled village. The letter describes Edward as dwelling in a hermitage in the castle of Cecima. Nor has there ever been a religious house there, but

Monastery of Sant' Alberto di Butrio, Edward's alleged second refuge in Italy.

five miles away was the monastery of Sant' Alberto di Butrio, often referred to as being at Cecima.

The village itself, its walls enclosing no more than six or seven acres, was not the sort of place where an ex-king of England could have lived unnoticed as a recluse but Sant' Alberto could have offered seclusion. From Cecima a by-road leads up into the still unspoilt and sparsely inhabited tracts of the Vogherese Appenines. Above the chestnut groves of the valleys the old monastery stands on a mountain spur at a height of more than two thousand feet, shut in by still higher slopes where clearings and alpine pastures scented with thyme and rosemary afford a meagre diet for the peasants' cattle and sheep. Even today it remains solitary and isolated; in medieval times reached only by stony paths and often cut off by snow in winter it could well have been the hiding place sought by a fugitive king.

Once a flourishing Benedictine monastery, it was more or less abandoned in the sixteenth century; today, as the Hermitage of Sant' Alberto it is the home of a religious brotherhood whose members devote their lives to prayer and labour. Within its walls are three Romanesque churches, two of which have fifteenth century frescoes in a remarkably good state of preservation. Should any reader find himself or herself near Genoa or Pavia on a spring or summer day Sant' Alberto, in the Michelin phrase, is well worth a detour.

The monastic records of the abbey from 1317 to 1400 have disappeared, so there is no information from that source, but in one of the three churches of Sant' Alberto, there are features that in the view of some Italian historians have a bearing on the contents of the letter. On the west side of the church is an open cloister some fifty yards in length. Behind its ten pillared arches lies a single tomb roughly carved out of rock, rather more than six feet long, two and a half feet wide and about two feet high. Above it is an arch without decoration or ornament save for two places for candle holders. In the Museo Civico del Arte in Turin are two large candlesticks of fourteenth century Limoges red and turquoise enamel work. They are said to have come from Sant' Alberto. On the base of each are two lions rampant; it has been suggested that they may have been presented to the monastery by Edward III. In his time Limoges was in the English king's Duchy of Aquitaine.

In the cloister and elsewhere there are carved capitals that have been identified as references to the tragedy of Edward II. One depicts a lion attacking a crowned king, and other a woman looking at the head of an

The Cloister at Sant' Alberto, in which is Edward's reputed tomb.

executed man and many others. At that time in Italy it was customary to depict scenes from the life of an important person at the place of his burial. It is tempting to draw inferences from these, but to this writer these carvings have a crudeness more typical of the eleventh century, when Sant' Alberto was founded, than of the fourteenth.

Every year on the first Sunday in September a festival takes place at Sant' Alberto when peasants, foresters and nowadays many pilgrims from outside the valley congregate. Professor Benedetti asserted that older people in the local population knew of the tradition that an English king had taken refuge there and that the festival was associated with this memory. Critics have suggested that the belief arose only after publicity had been given to Germain's discovery of the letter. However, in 1958 enquiries among the peasants found that there were many older people who had been told about the king by parents and grandparents, taking the tradition back into the nineteenth century, before Constantine Nigra had linked the story to Sant' Alberto.

None of this adds up to proof that Edward's last years were spent in Italy, though there is nothing inherently improbable about his alleged desire to turn his back on the world. The events of 1327 were enough to break any man's spirit; his wife had deserted and betrayed him, his closest friends had been hideously put to death and not a single voice had been raised in Parliament to protest against his imprisonment.

Many questions still remain unanswered. If the story of his second escape were true, how could it have remained unknown for five hundred years? Even if the Pope had agreed to keep it secret, such a sensational arrival at his court must have been known to many others. For example, Adam of Orleton, Bishop of Worcester, who had led the delegation sent to Kenilworth to secure Edward's abdication, was at Avignon for six months in 1332. As head of an embassy he travelled with a retinue of clerics and laymen and a military escort. It was not his first visit; he was persona grata with Pope John who on this occasion nominated him to the more important see of Winchester. It is inconceivable that he would not have been told or heard gossip of Edward's visit or that all members of his staff should have remained in ignorance. Some contemporary English chronicler would surely have heard of it and recorded or hinted at such an amazing story.

One Italian writer does indeed say that an official from Berkeley visited Avignon in 1330 and on return to England reported that Pope John knew

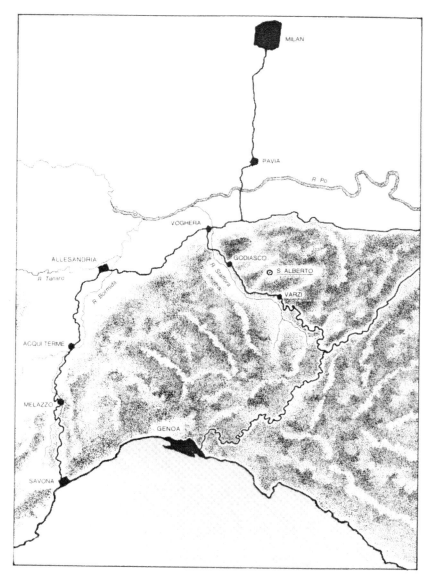

Melazzo and Sant' Alberto di Butrio, Ligurian Apennines.

that Edward was alive, but I have been unable to find any confirmation of this statement. It may be the result of a confusion with Bishop Orleton's visit two years later, since he had links with the tragedy and also with Berkeley, but again I do not know that he ever said anything like that.

As Bishop Stubbs, the great nineteenth century historian pointed out, whenever a medieval king met with a mysterious or violent end, rumours about his survival in some remote place always began to circulate among the credulous. But we are dealing here not with a widely held belief but with a detailed account told by a single person. On balance the reader will probably have concluded that although the letter may be genuine it is difficult to accept the truth of the escape story. However, we should not dismiss it as unworthy of further attention. When we have traced the fortunes of the conspirators over the years that followed, the purpose and significance of Fieschi's letter should emerge.

CHAPTER EIGHT

UNEASY INTERLUDE

Treason doth never prosper.

SIR J. HARINGTON

On the fall of Edward a Council of Regency was set up to govern the kingdom during the young king's minority. Mortimer was not a member; this was unnecessary. Isabel used all her authority to further her lover's ambition; within a few months she and Mortimer had taken control of the government. She was able to dominate her son. As for the future, she may have hoped that he would grow into a man like his father, content to leave the business of the kingdom to others. If so, she was mistaken.

One of the first steps taken was to reverse the judgements of the Despenser period. Parliament duly declared that the rebellion of Thomas of Lancaster and the barons was justified; the lands and possessions of all who had taken part were restored. For those barons and knights who had died on the scaffold this was postumous "rehabilitation" of the kind so common in Eastern Europe in our own day; no help to the liquidated in any age, but in the fourteenth century of considerable importance to widows and children, who thus regained the family estates.

So Thomas, Lord Berkeley did homage and received again his castle and manors. He was pardoned for all "robberies, murders and felonies" committed by him. He lost no time in claiming recompense for the damage done to his possessions by the Despensers. The jewels and money taken from the castle were found in the London house of the Bardi, Edward II's Italian bankers, when the queen confiscated their wealth. But Thomas got back only half of what had been taken; Isabel, never one to miss the chance of adding to her own wealth, kept the rest as reward for her part in its recovery.

After all this had been settled Thomas returned to Berkeley where, according to John Smyth, he found that his granges, manor houses and farm buildings were so out of repair and damaged that for the next two years an army of carpenters, masons and tylers were occupied in putting things right. As he had been in prison at the time of his father's death and the estates forfeit to the Crown, he had never taken possession of his inheritance. Courts were at once held in all his thirty manors whose inhabitants were obliged to express their joy in their lord's return by making "recognition" payments of from fourteen to twenty shillings. The careful supervision and precise accounting characteristic of his manors were soon restored.

The Berkeleys and their friends now prospered under the Mortimer regime. Thomas's younger brother Maurice had come out of four years in hiding to join Isabel's invading army; he was soon in possession of his share of the family manors. Maurice was also given custody of the extensive and profitable Despenser manors of Tewkesbury and Sodbury and of the city and castle of Gloucester. His later appointments as Keeper of Bristol Castle and Constable of the Tower of London show how Mortimer trusted him.

Thomas had an uncle, James Berkeley, a doctor of divinity of Oxford who had often been employed by Edward II on diplomatic missions to the Pope. In the usual way he enjoyed a good income from the numerous livings, canonries and archdeaconries that had been conferred on him. Now he was a candidate for a more distinguished and lucrative office. In March 1327, on the order of Isabel he was consecrated Bishop of Exeter. Unfortunately for James he did not live long enough to enjoy the revenues of his bishopric, dying a few months later. Though never officially canonised, James thereafter had a local reputation as a saint, on grounds not specified. Thomas on the anniversary of his uncle's death went to Exeter, offered at his tomb and gave alms to all the religious houses of the city. Insurance, perhaps, against possible changes of fortune.

Sir John Maltravers, as one would expect, was in high favour. He was given most of the lands of the executed John Giffard of Brimpsfield, who had left no heir. As governor of Corfe Castle he lorded it over his native Dorset; as Keeper of the Forests South of the Trent he received an enviable income. Before long he became Steward of the Household, escorting the young king on a state visit to France. Finally, in 1330 a writ of summons to Parliament established him in the ranks of the baronage as John, Lord Maltravers.

Sir Thomas Gournay was less generously rewarded with the governorship of Bristol, but of course he regained his forfeited Somerset estates. William of Ocle's special services were recognised by the gift of the rich Cheshire manor of Ellesmere. But these two, who are reputed to have played sinister parts in the tragedy, remained in the background during the years of Mortimer rule.

That wily Berkeley retainer, Thomas de Bradestone, who had kept possession of his two little manors through all the troubles (joining in the Baron's Revolt, making his peace with the Despensers, buying his liberty from Edward and changing sides adroitly when Isabel appeared) now began another career as a courtier. He became a Gentleman of the Privy Chamber and was soon rewarded with many profitable wardships and offices. Then in 1330 he aspired to knighthood, receiving the custody of Gloucester for the better maintenance of his new rank.

By the spring of 1328 Thomas, Lord Berkeley had made good progress in the restoration of his castle. Not until then was he able to bring home his young wife, Margaret Mortimer, whom he had married seven unhappy years before on the eve of the Despenser war. We do not know what her feelings were towards her husband, or whether she found the castle an agreeable home. No doubt a girl from the border lands had heard enough talk of violence and sudden death to accept these as normal hazards of political life. The people of the Honour of Berkeley did their best to give her the customary "joyous incoming" with a gift of three pounds nineteen shillings and sixpence in gold. They perhaps would have been ready and able to give more had they not suffered at the hands of both sides.

In contrast to these humble offerings, Roger Mortimer was now able to hand over the splendid dowry of £850 that he had at the time of the marriage contracted to pay. Long delays of this kind were quite usual in normal times: the past seven years had been far from normal.

It must have been this money that enabled Thomas to begin the rebuilding of his castle for Margaret's better accommodation. The old Norman hall was replaced by a handsome one in the fashionable Decorated style; the gatehouses were rebuilt to give a more impressive entry. For his own pleasures Thomas enclosed an extensive new deer park with another fine gatehouse. Over the Severn at Awre, on the estate that he had been given by Mortimer, he built a manor house. From the forest of Michaelwood three score great oak trees were shipped across the river. Thomas was on excellent terms with his father-in-law and the party in power. He often sent thoughtful little gifts to his relatives and patrons; a dish of pears to his neglected mother-in-law at Wigmore, a few lamprey pies or a Severn porpoise to the queen who had replaced her in Mortimer's affections.

After the embarrassing failure of 1327 Roger Mortimer did not venture to mount another major expedition against the Scots. Instead he hoped to win popularity and give the barons an outlet for their martial energies by a series of splendid tournaments. He began with an elaborately staged Round Table at Bedford, as spectacular as the famous Kenilworth meeting organised by his grandfather, when an earlier Maurice de Berkeley had been killed. Though Bedford was a success, an unwise heraldic display drawing attention to Mortimer's descent from a Welsh prince led to suspicions and whisperings.

Later in that summer of 1328 two of his daughters were married, ceremonies marked by two more Round Tables at his castles of Wigmore and Ludlow, occasions of magnificence and lavish entertainment remarkable even for the fourteenth century.

On the way to Wigmore, Mortimer and Isabel with their retinue of courtiers, officials and servants came to stay at Berkeley. Why did they come? Morbid curiosity? So that Isabel might still suspicion by appearing as a sorrowing widow? Whatever the reason, the memory of the murdered king cast no shadow of gloom over the visit, during which Lord de Clifford was married to another Isabel, Thomas's sister, in that chapel of St. John where oblations were still being offered for Edward's soul. The queen and her lover must have been strangely devoid of any feeling of guilt or compassion. One suspects that Isabel's infatuation with her Marcher lord was such that she had ceased to think at all about the man who was the father of her children.

After six days of hunting, hawking and festivity the queen and her party moved on from Berkeley in good spirits. Thomas, his brother and his knights rode with them along the familiar border roads, in the past to war, now to share in the pageantry and excitement of its substitute. But at Wigmore and Ludlow the ostentation of Mortimer's display and his royal bearing, far from winning popularity, antagonised many of the barons. Their hostility was shown openly when it was announced that he had been created Earl of March.

The earls, traditionally the king's closest advisers, were always jealous of the admission of newcomers to their rank. Earls were from time to time created, but almost always from those who had achieved military distinction. Hence the deep dislike of Gaveston and the elder Despenser.

Moreover, the title was particularly offensive to all the many barons who held lands in the Marches. No one had ever held an earldom of March, with its implied overlordship of all the Marcher barons, who were firecely tenacious of their special relationship with the Crown, and in their own lands did not acknowledge the authority even of the king's officials. Their suspicions were increased by Mortimer's acquisitions. He was no politician or skilled administrator. For him, his position of power was just an opportunity to make himself rich. He had inherited his uncle's lands around Chirk Castle; now he gave himself custody of all those Despenser lands in Glamorgan that had been a chief cause of the revolt of 1321. To these he added all the manors of the Earl of Arundel, executed for his support of Edward II, and the Justiciarship of Wales. No Marcher had ever possessed so much, but still he was not satisfied. Isabel was just as greedy for wealth.

When Parliament met at Salisbury in the autumn of 1328 many barons came with bands of armed retainers. There were disorders that should have been a warning to Mortimer. In the new year Henry of Lancaster joined with some of the barons in asking that the Council of Regency should be given more power to govern and, more ominously, that the young king should be given a separate household.

Mortimer's answer to these reasonable requests was a display of force. Henry's estates were seized, alarming a number of barons who went into hiding or left the country. Henry paid a heavy fine for his pardon, but Mortimer decided that it was necessary to make an example of someone. For this he chose the Earl of Kent, Edward's half-brother, a young man of no political importance who had talked to Henry. He became a victim of an elaborate and cunning plot.

The instrument chosen was John Maltravers. He was so deeply compromised that another murder would not make much difference to his future if things should go wrong. Indeed, he may not have had much choice about the role for which he was cast.

Maltravers informed the earl that Edward was still alive, in captivity at Corfe. Kent fell for the story; a friar of his household was sent down to Dorset to investigate. In lay dress he obtained entry to the castle by bribing the porter at the gate and hid in the lodge. The porter had been given his

Corfe Castle, Dorset.

instructions. That night Maltravers and his accomplices staged an elaborate pageant "using many lights to make shows with dancing and masking upon the towers and walls". All this was seen by the friar who later was allowed to watch the scene in the great hall when a fair haired bearded man who looked like the late king was entertained royally at supper, attended by many servants.

The friar returned and reported to the earl, who thereupon wrote letters to several friends. The letters were intercepted, Kent was arrested and hurriedly brought to trial before Parliament in March, 1330. It is unnecessary to add that he was convicted of treason and immediately executed. One can only marvel at the willingness of the barons, throughout English history, to condemn their peers at the demand of the government of the day. Presumably, failure to agree to a verdict of guilty would mark the dissenter himself as a treasonable character. To draw a parallel, the findings of "People's Courts" of our own day are always unanimous.

By this action Mortimer had overreached himself. His conduct hastened his downfall. "He was held in such honour and glory that it was without all comparison", wrote a chronicler. "No man durst name him other than Earl of March" (that is, instead of the customary Sir Roger) and a greater rout of men walked on his heels than on the king's person. He would suffer the king to rise to him and would walk equally with him, step by step, never preferring the king, but would go foremost himself with his officers". The barons were sure that he intended to place himself on the throne.

Under the surface plans to overthrow Mortimer were being made. At this point a new and important figure appears. William Montagu, a youngish member of the king's retinue, had never been involved in the troubles of the previous reign. An articulate and intelligent man, in close attendance upon the king, he was able to tell him the views of the younger barons. Edward, now come of age, was already quite capable of thinking for himself and proud enough to resent Mortimer's behaviour. Nor could he have been blind to the relationship between Mortimer and his mother. They were openly living together, "sharing a common purse". Edward found himself in a position not dissimilar to that of Hamlet. Unlike the Prince of Denmark he was uninhibited by doubt or hesitation and quick to end a situation which seemed to him shameful.

Parliament was summoned to meet at Nottingham. Thomas, Lord Berkeley rode there with the new made peer, John Maltravers, thus rewarded for his ugly services. Montagu and his friends had decided that this was their opportunity. At night they broke into Nottingham Castle by way of an underground passage, seized Mortimer and killed or arrested his guards. This was done in the presence of the young king, who had awaited Montagu in the castle courtyard. Next day Roger Mortimer was taken to imprisonment in the Tower of London. This time there were no friends inside or outside the walls ready and capable of helping him to escape.

CHAPTER NINE

A FAIRLY CLEAN SLATE

Whatever you do, do cautiously,
and look to the end.

GESTA ROMANORUM

The overthrow of Mortimer left a politically difficult situation. Not only the queen but many barons, bishops and lesser men had been involved in the dethronement of Edward II; too close a scrutiny of their actions would weaken the support needed by the new government. A public investigation of the circumstances of his death might well implicate the queen.

These problems were lessened by sending Isabel away into comfortable, even luxurious retirement at Castle Rising; she was never permitted to appear again at court. This made it possible to deal separately with Mortimer. When Parliament met on 5th November at Westminster he was brought before a joint sitting of both Houses. Fourteen treasons, felonies and misdemeanours were alleged against him. He was accused of having caused the father of the king to be murdered, but no details were given. Much more emphasis was laid on the judicial murder of the Earl of Kent. No reference was made to his liaison with the queen; it was merely said that he had given evil counsel to her and the young king "to his dishonour and the ruin of the kingdom and Holy Church". For good measure he was accused of taking bribes from the Scots in return for allowing them to escape in the campaign of 1327, a preposterous charge which, however, shows how deeply that failure rankled in the minds of king and barons.

No evidence was offered in support of any charges, nor was Mortimer heard in his own defence. His crimes were declared to be notorious, as indeed some of them were. We have seen that this was normal procedure when dealing with rebel barons, but it seems that Edward III wished to make it clear to all that this was not to be just another execution merely at the king's command. A small commission of justices and barons was set up to consider the charges and recommend appropriate punishment. They proposed that Mortimer should be hung, drawn and quartered—the barbarous practice imported from the continent and used for the Despensers.

Parliament met again in January; the king charged the earls and barons to pronounce upon Mortimer the judgement proper for one guilty of his crimes; the suggested sentence was confirmed by them. Thus, care had been taken to show that an acceptable judicial procedure had been followed, in contrast to the summary executions of recent years.

On the scaffold Mortimer made some amends by admitting that the Earl of Kent had not been guilty of treason, but said nothing about the death of Edward II. He met his death with the impassivity expected of a baron. On the order of the king the ghastly business of disembowelling, burning and carving up was omitted; the body was sent home for burial at Wigmore. It was almost exactly four years since, in Mortimer's presence, Hugh Despenser had been butchered at Hereford.

There followed no savage slaughter of all those who had been led by hatred of the Despensers to replace Edward II by his son, only to find themselves propping up an equally self-seeking administration. The young king did not wish to bring into existence another group of disaffected barons waiting an opportunity for revenge. The only associate of Mortimer to be executed was the somewhat shadowy Sir Simon de Barford. In his case there was no mention of complicity in the murder at Berkeley, though he was there at the time and was later named as one of the assassins. It was the government's aim to avoid publicity. Barford had been one of Mortimer's men on the Council of Regency and this was used to justify a charge of treason.

During the months when he had been organising the coup Montagu had apparently gathered some information about the identity of the actual murderers. It could only have come from someone in the Berkeley circle. However, it does not seem that any arrangements had been made to arrest the guilty men. Not until early December did the king send writs to all sheriffs telling them that William of Ocle, Sir Thomas Gournay and others who had been charged with "diverse offences" were trying to leave the realm. They were to be arrested and brought before the king. They were not caught. With the exception of Thomas, Lord Berkeley, the chief actors in the tragedy and several minor figures vanished from sight on the fall of Mortimer.

John Maltravers had been at Nottingham but he got away in the confusion of the night, riding hard to the West Country to carry the news to Berkeley and no doubt to warn Thomas Gournay in Somerset. By Christmas both had crossed the Channel. William of Ocle is also said to have gone abroad, but he was never heard of again. Possibly he was killed to ensure his silence. He was not a Berkeley, nor was he of knightly rank, so he was expendable. He may have been killed out of hand by government agents.

After Mortimer had been charged, Gournay and William of Ocle were in their absence accused of "falsely and traitorously murdering the father of the king". No evidence was offered before they were sentenced to death. Maltravers was charged with helping to bring about the murder of Edward and also that of the Earl of Kent "by falsely pretending that the former king was alive when he knew that he was dead". He was sentenced to death by hanging and beheading; his estates were confiscated; he was outlawed and a thousand marks offered for his capture alive.

And what of Thomas Lord Berkeley? He was not arrested at Nottingham, since he was at Berkeley when he received his writ of summons to the Westminster Parliament in November, appearing before it to answer charges. The case against him looked black. Whereas King Edward, father of the king, had been delivered to his custody and that of Sir John Maltravers, to be safely kept by them in Berkeley Castle and since he had been murdered there whilst in his custody, how could he acquit himself of the king's death?

Thomas, like some modern propagandists, evidently believed that a big lie is more likely to be successful than a little one. "He answered that he was neither knowing, helping nor procuring thereto, nor ever knew thereof until the present Parliament, whereof he was ready to acquit himself as this Parliament should command". In short, this was the first he had heard of this regrettable affair.

He was told plainly that as lord of the castle he had accepted the king to be safely kept, so he must answere for his death. To this Thomas replied that at the time of Edward's death he was at his manor of Bradley, near Wotton-under-Edge. Here he was taken ill. In fact his condition was so serious that his life was despaired of; he had in consequence lost all memory of the events of that time. Sickness afforded no excuse, said his accusers, brushing this aside. He had appointed the immediate gaolers, so he must accept responsibility for their actions.

Thomas answered again that he had placed, under Maltravers, keepers and servants whom he trusted as much as in himself. This plea disposes of the story that he had been relieved of his duties by Mortimer and ordered to hand over to Maltravers and Gournay. This tale must have been invented by someone who wished to minimise Thomas's part in the affair. Finally, Thomas repeated that he was not guilty of Edward's death; he therefore put himself upon his country—that is, he submitted himself to the judgement of reputable men of his own district.

Inexplicably, Thomas's plea was accepted. Normally, a baron accused of treasonable activities was sentenced by judgment of his peers, after the usual recital of the alleged facts by the king, in Parliament. But in this instance the king ordered that the matter should stand over until the next Parliament. In the meantime, Thomas would be committed to the custody of Ralph de Nevill, Steward of the Household. In modern terms, he was released on bail.

Only a few weeks elapsed before Parliament met again, in January—when Mortimer was finally sentenced. The jury of twelve knights had been empanelled, equally from Gloucestershire and Warwickshire, from the latter county because Thomas had received Edward into his custody at Kenilworth. It occurs to one that it could have been difficult to find knights in Gloucestershire who were not in some way linked with the Berkeleys, whilst those from Warwickshire could not possibly have known anything about the circumstances of the murder.

We do not know what enquiries were made or what evidence was heard. Did the knights simply act as witnesses to character, giving it as their opinion that Thomas was not the man to commit such a crime? There were men at Berkeley who must have known a great deal, but would they have dared to give testimony that would harm their lord? There is no evidence that any enquiries were made there.

However that may be, the jury, upon their oaths, found that Lord Thomas was not guilty, that he was at his manor of Bradley at the time of the murder, so sick that it was expected he would die. Nor did they find that he had deliberately absented himself from his castle because of the impending crime.

The jury's very favourable verdict did not bring an immediate acquittal for Thomas. Even if it were accepted, the ugly facts remained: the murder had been committed in his castle and he had failed to ensure the victim's safety. Giving himself time for consideration, the king took no action, beyond requiring Thomas to appear at the next Parliament. Evidently he had plenty of friends among the barons and bishops, who petitioned the king that he should be released from his bail. This the king was pleased to grant, so Thomas returned to Berkeley more or less as a free man, though still, so to speak, on probation.

Before he left Westminster Thomas requested that the king should pay him the £600 still owing in respect of his father's governorship of Berwick, held some fourteen years ago. His dangerous predicament had not impaired his self-assurance. His petition was granted, though it was years later that he got the money.

For six more years Thomas continued in attendance at each succeeding parliament, awaiting the king's pleasure. In 1335 Edward charged the magnates assembled at York to advise whether Thomas Berkeley was guilty of the king's father's death or whether he was "assenting or procuring thereto". They replied that they held that he was not guilty, but, obviously reluctant to take final responsibility themselves, referred the matter to the king. Edward then also acquitted him but reserved "the right to dispose of him by Parliament hereafter, by common counsel and advice". Not until 1337 was he finally and formally acquitted by King in Parliament and even then, though they adjudged him free "henceforth and for ever", they added "saving some fault of negligence".

This final judgment reflects the king's clemency to one who was already giving good service. During the years of probation, when the ball was being thrown to and fro between the king and the barons, Thomas was given plenty of employment, civil and military. In 1332 he was present at Edward's victory over the Scots at Halidon Hill, with his usual quota of knights and troopers and 500 Gloucestershire footmen he had raised at the king's request. In the year of his acquittal he was again in Scotland. True to the Berkeley tradition, he took his seven year old son with him; Margaret Mortimer had just died.

That jury of knights, whoever they were, saved Thomas's life and barony for him, but those good men and true must have made a very perfunctory examination of the circumstances of the crime. John Smyth, loyal as he was to his Berkeley masters, was scrupulous in his handling of the family history. He points out that Thomas could not possibly have been at Bradley on 20th September, since his household accounts show that he did not arrive there until seven days later. Nor could he have been so ill that he lost his memory, for on 22nd September he wrote the letter giving news of Edward's death, sent to Mortimer by the hand of Gournay. Furthermore, he received Mortimer's order and kept the death secret until All Saints Day. Finally, on the fall of Mortimer he concealed Gournay and helped him to escape. Smyth even suggests that Gournay was chosen to be the bearer of the letter so that he could be blamed for the crime if things went wrong. He was quite sure that Thomas was deeply implicated, observing that no one could ever know what verbal instructions passed between Mortimer and his son-in-law.

Lord Thomas's escape was indeed remarkable. Several questions call for answers. Why was he not immediately arrested at Nottingham? Why was he not summarily sentenced at Westminster, like Barford, Maltravers, Ocle and Gournay? Why was he, a peer, allowed to put himself upon his country, to be judged by a group of more or less local knights—a procedure that had no precedent?

His own skill helped to ensure his survival, but he must have had powerful friends. One small piece of evidence points to this. Within two years of Edward's murder he had struck up a friendship with William Montagu, who made him a present of white deer for his park at Berkeley. The friendship continued. When Thomas gave the great east window in what is now Bristol Cathedral, the arms of Montague were placed among those of the Berkeleys and their allies. Is it possible that Thomas had thrown in his lot with Montagu and had foreknowledge of what was to happen at Nottingham Castle? Was it Thomas himself who supplied Montagu with the names of the actual murderers? This is conjecture, but it would explain why Thomas was handled so gently after the coup.

At the time when Thomas was awaiting the verdict of the knights he took the precaution of founding and endowing a chapel at Wortley, a hamlet near his manor house at Wotton-under-Edge. There a priest was established to pray for him and his heirs, in life and in death, in all the masses and orisons said there. This may have helped, but Thomas was one of those who believe that Heaven helps those who help themselves. Smyth, poring over the family papers, remarked that "they manifestly showed with what art this lord shuffled his cards".

The last earl of Berkeley, dining with an Indian prince, told him the story. "Why?" asked the astonished prince, "Why weren't all the Berkeleys exterminated at once? In India, if you had murdered a maharajah, you wouldn't have had a chance".

During the weeks after Mortimer's downfall, when he himself was in grave danger, Lord Thomas was secretly helping his accomplices to leave the country. It was very much in his interest that they should escape. Maltravers had fled from Nottingham to warn Maurice Berkeley who, it will be recalled, was an old hand at concealment, having been a fugitive during the years of Despenser rule, Maurice had not been implicated in the murder. He now arranged with the abbot of Malmesbury, one of his former protectors, to hide Maltravers in the monastery until the hunt died down. Then Maurice and another Berkeley knight, Sir William de Whitefield, took him down to Cornwall. From there he crossed to Brittany and made his way to the Low Countries.

Sir Thomas Gournay was also hidden away during the critical weeks after his outlawry. It is likely that Lord Thomas put him aboard one of the many ships trading between Bristol and Bordeaux, perhaps on the one that he himself owned. At all events, Gournay turned up in Spain. Thomas furnished the money for his travels. In return for this the fugitive gave him a carefully undated lease and letters of attorney for Gournay manors in Gloucestershire, for his and his wife's lives. So long as Thomas could clear himself of complicity in the crime this would save Gournay's lands from forfeiture to the Crown. Some of the income from them could be passed on, and no doubt was.

Gournay, however, was a marked man. Edward III, though he did not wish to stir up too much mud, was apparently determined to run to earth those most closely involved in his father's death. When news of Gournay's presence in Spain reached the English court, Edward asked the King of Castile to keep a lookout for him. Soon afterwards he was arrested at Burgos by a Spanish nobleman. Edward sent out an English knight with a reward of £300 for the captor. Although this was paid the Spanish government made difficulties about extradition; Gournay was allowed to slip away.

In 1332 came news that he was in Italy. Edward was able to get him arrested in Naples; again an escort was sent to bring him home. Gournay and his guards landed at Marseilles and travelled across Languedoc and Gascony to Bayonne. His escort's expenses sheet shows payments for "medicines", so he may have been in poor health after his wanderings. The party took ship from Bayonne to Bordeaux. On the way Gournay died; the chronicler Murimuth says that he was beheaded at sea. Others have suggested that he was poisoned by those medicines.

However he died, it was very convenient. Two years had passed since the execution of Mortimer; Gournay's arrival in England would have been a reminder of unhappy events just when divisions were beginning to heal; there were signs that the baronage was again to be united under the leadership of a popular soldier king. Certainly Lord Thomas must have slept more easily, for Gournay was a man who could have incriminated him beyond all hope of acquittal.

John Maltravers fared better. In the Low Countries and Germany it was easy for a knight to find employment. As this was his second period of exile he had plenty of contacts. In time, Edward III learned of his presence there but no attempt was made to get him arrested. His friends at home were active on his behalf. Maurice Berkeley obtained from the king a grant of all the castles, manors and lands in England that had been given to Maltravers from the Giffard estates. A year afterwards there was added to this "all his goods and chattels in whose hands soever these may be". Maurice was to hold these for life with reversion to Maltravers's son. The baronage looked after its own as efficiently as any modern old boy network. Though errant or unfortunate members might suffer death and loss of lands their dependents did not starve. Rich merchants might move up into the ranks of the nobility but there was little traffic in the other direction. No doubt some of the Maltravers revenue found its way to the exile in Flanders.

After a few years he made an approach to the English government, perhaps indicating that he might be prepared to throw some light on the murder. As a result of this William Montagu was sent to interview him. Maltravers impressed him by his knowledge of Flemish affairs. Edward III, already contemplating war as a means of making good his claim to the French throne, was anxious to bring about alliances with the Duke of Brabant and Jacob van Artevelde, the Captain-general of Ghent. Montagu realised that Maltravers could help with this business. The outlawed exile thus became an unofficial agent of the English government, receiving a grant of £100 when Artevelde agreed to support Edward in the event of a war with France. Other diplomatic employment followed, including an unexplained mission to Ireland 'on the king's business". From that time there began a lengthy process of political rehabilitation.

At this point it is worth considering again the Italian priest's letter. Almost a century ago Bishop Stubbs, speculating about its origin, made several suggestions. One was that it might have been the pretended confession of someone well-acquainted with the facts of the crime and deeply implicated, who hatched a plan to save himself from the consequences. If we adopt this hypothesis it is not difficult to find a man who fills the bill.

First, let us try to estimate when the undated letter was written. The Earl of Kent was executed early in 1330. Fieschi says that Edward left Corfe Castle at about that time, in which case he would be in Ireland until near the end of the year. This would mean that he would cross England on his way to Sandwich soon after Mortimer's fall, reaching Avignon by February or March 1331. His stay with the Pope and his pilgrimage to Cologne would occupy most of the remaining months of that year. If so, he would have reached Melazzo early in 1332, moving on from there in the summer or autumn of 1334 after a stay of two and a half years. His death at Sant' Alberto would then have occurred in late 1336.

This time sequence must have been in the mind of whoever 'confessed' to Manuele del Fieschi, so it follows that the letter could not have been written before 1337, which is the year when Manuele became a Papal secretary at Avignon. It also happens to be the year when the rehabilitation of John Maltravers began to get under way with his employment as a government agent.

The person who 'confessed' to Manuele is not named but clearly he was someone who had been at Berkeley when Edward was imprisoned there, had been in some way involved and was now living in exile. Maltravers was the only surviving fugitive of whom this was true.

We have seen that Manuele was quite probably at the English court in 1329 when Maltravers was Steward of the Household and that the two may well have become acquainted. Indeed the tone of the letter seems to suggest that Manuele would be known to the king. Did Maltravers, wishing to help on his reconciliation with the English government, get in touch with Manuele persuading him to send the pretended confession which would exonerate him from complicity in the intended crime.

The letter names two men who were safely dead as the would-be murderers, Gournay and Barford. This was the first time that Barford had been mentioned as one of the guilty men; he was not charged with murder when he was arrested and executed. Suspicion lay most heavily on Gournay and Maltravers, the two deputy governors, both of whom had fled the country. The king's favourable treatment of Maltravers has always been hard to explain. Was the story told in the letter one of the reasons why Montagu went over to Flanders to meet him? And that mysterious journey to Ireland 'on the king's business': did Maltravers go to find 'evidence' of Edward's brief exile there?

One can picture Maltravers and Manuele concocting the letter, the former supplying details of the alleged escape and the priest placing Edward's refuges in that part of Italy of which he had personal knowledge, for the Fieschi family belonged to Genoa and in fact Manuele later on became bishop of Vercelli, a town not more than forty miles distant from Sant' Alberto.

It may also be significant that it was in 1337 that Thomas Lord Berkeley was finally acquitted by King and Parliament of any complicity in the murder. Of course it is true that we have no proof that the letter ever reached the king; Professor Germain discovered only a secretary's copy or draft. No original has ever been found in England, nor any reference to its arrival here but Edward III and his advisers, who had from the beginning done nothing to end the secrecy first imposed by Isabel and Mortimer, were not willing to open the closed book ten years later.

If indeed Edward III did receive Fieschi's letter the king's silence and absence of action would have been prudent. After all, he had erected the magnificent canopy over his father's tomb at Gloucester, had himself gone there with his queen to hear mass many times as had thousands of pilgrims; to announce that his father's body did not lie there would have been embarrassing, to say the least. If the letter arrived he might not have believed the story of the escape but he would perhaps have used it to justify in his own mind his lenient treatment of the two surviving conspirators, both of whom were giving him good service. For our part, we need not doubt the old Berkeley squire's account of the end of Edward II: 'they shortened his life for him'.

CHAPTER TEN

THE ART OF SURVIVAL

Great families are noted to be as stages,
whereon are represented the vicissitudes of
various fortunes.

JOHN SMYTH: LIVES OF THE BERKELEYS

Two months after Thomas Berkeley's final acquittal his wife, Margaret Mortimer, died when barely thirty years of age. For the widower there was no respite from duty. Fighting had broken out again along the borders of Gascony and the Scots, as allies of the French, were threatening to invade the north of England. Thomas was commissioned by the king as his sole lieutenant in the counties of Gloucester, Worcester and Hereford to raise forces for service in England and France, a task that occupied him for the summer months. Then after a brief foray into Somerset to repress disorders that the sheriff and justices had failed to deal with, he set off again on the long march to Carlisle.

In the Berkeley tradition he took with him his seven year old eldest son, another Maurice. Nearly all Berkeley boys went to war early in life, but this one earlier than most. Before he returned at the end of the year the child had been knighted by his father on the battlefield and dedicated to a lifetime of warfare that only ended twenty-four years later when he was crippled and taken prisoner in the battle of Poitiers.

Although Thomas has been cleared 'henceforth and for ever' he could not be entirely easy about the future. There was always the possibility that the heirs of Hugh Despenser who had been granted the Berkeley manors and castle by Edward II and had held them for six years might one day dispute his possession. Charters of award and restoration were complex and sometimes ambiguous, offering opportunities to lawyers who were expert at finding flaws in title. Every prudent baron maintained his private council of chaplain-lawyers who function was not only to defend their master's manors but to probe the legal rights of other barons, seeking a chance to bring a successful action. Territorial claims were nourished for generations, awaiting the right moment for renewal.

Almost immediately the danger became acute. In 1338 Hugh Despenser's son (yet another Hugh) was restored to favour as part of Edward III's policy of all-round conciliation. He was summoned to Parliament as a baron and most of the family estates were restored to him.

The accepted method of anticipating baronial claims was to arrange a dynastic marriage, so little Maurice, safely returned from his first campaign, was married to the granddaughter of Hugh, the hated despoiler of the Berkeley manors whose execution Thomas had watched with such satisfaction at Hereford. No matter, the young man who succeeded to the Berkeley estates in 1368 was a Despenser-Berkeley and for good measure had Roger Mortimer as his grandfather.

The marriage turned out to be a wise precaution. Edward Despenser, the next baron, came to Berkeley in 1365 with Jean Froissart who recorded his bitter complaint about Queen Isabel's action in depriving his family of such a splendid inheritance.

No vassal gave Edward III more faithful service than Thomas Berkeley. When the king's claim to the French throne sparked off the struggle that we know as the Hundred Years' War, Thomas was guaranteed full martial employment for the rest of his life. In 1340 he was commandeering ships in the Bristol Channel for Edward's expedition to Flanders and in that campaign he appears not only as 'a most able sea-captain' but as Marshal of the large army carried by the ships that won the battle of Sluys. Next we hear of him as a witness to Edward's treaty with the Duke of Brabant, arranging the marriage of the future Black Prince to the Duke's daughter.

No sooner was Thomas back in England than he was marching to Scotland for another relief of Stirling Castle and in 1342 he was Warden of the Scottish Marches, inflicting a resounding defeat on a Scottish force commanded by Lord William Douglas. Two or three times each year he was called with other trusted barons to attend the king's council at Westminster or some other city; those dangerous months and years after the fall of Mortimer had been skilfully navigated. That he did not follow his father-in-law on the scaffold still surprises the historians.

His brother Maurice Berkeley and Thomas Bradestone, those 'sworn companions in arms', shared in all these campaigns as professional soldiers. Bradestone, the perpetual survivor, soon became a banneret with a pension of five hundred marks a year, contracted to accompany the king overseas whenever required with his own contingent of more than forty knights, troopers and archers. Good service was recognised by a knighthood and then in 1343 he reached the high point of his career when he was called to Parliament as a baron. In sixteen years this Berkeley tenant and man-at-arms had become a peer and risen to a military rank comparable, say, with that of a brigadier today.

All the Berkeleys and their friends were in Flanders in 1345, an unlucky year for Edward III, when the Brabant alliance collapsed. John Maltravers chose that moment to approach the king, who was at Sluys, to make his peace. Maltravers humbly submitted that he had been condemned and outlawed without a hearing—hardly surprising, since he had disappeared without waiting to be charged. Now, he said, he wished to return to England to be tried by his peers. He had been ennobled a few months before his flight, but he was ignoring the fact that his outlawry had deprived him of the rights and privileges of his peerage. What Edward really thought of this brazen impudence is not on record but Maltravers came back to England with the royal party.

Next year came the great expedition to Normandy. Maurice Berkeley, Bradestone and Maltravers were all with the army, sharing in the looting of the rich, almost undefended Norman towns. They went on to fight under the command of Edward and the Black Prince at Crecy but Thomas was not with them; he had remained at home as one of a small council of trusted barons charged with the defence of the kingdom against a possible French diversionary raid or a Scottish invasion.

In the following year Edward, besieging Calais, was threatened by an approaching French army. Thomas received an urgent summons to come at once bringing all the men-at-arms and archers he could gather, without waiting for horses. His response was immediate and effective. He arrived in Calais with six knights, thirty-two esquires, thirty mounted archers and two hundred footmen. The French attack did not come so Thomas returned to Berkeley, but his brother Maurice had died at Calais before the capture of the town.

After his service at Crecy and Calais John Maltravers continued to be employed by Edward III as soldier and diplomat though his actual status was still that of an outlaw under sentence of death. At last, in 1351 the conviction and outlawry were annulled and the king restored his estates (which had ever since been managed by Thomas Berkeley) and called him to Parliament again as a baron. It had taken this man, widely credited with the actual murder of Edward II, twenty-one years to work his way back.

So the Berkeleys and their allies prospered in the employment of the king. It is intriguing to picture the three barons, Thomas Berkeley, Bradestone and Maltravers together riding up to Parliament at Westminster. They certainly did not lack subjects for conversation but one doubts if they ever said much about the events of the night of 21st September, 1327.

The climax of Thomas Berkeley's military career came in 1355. He, his son Maurice, Bradestone and Maltravers returned to Gascony this time accompanying the Black Prince on his appointment as governor and commander-in-chief of Aquitaine. With him they went on the march to the Loire that ended in the great but barren victory of Poitiers.

There were three hundred Gloucestershire men on that battlefield; a dozen Berkeleys, their feudal allies and the humble footmen from the villages of the Severn Vale. Maurice Berkeley, the child whom Thomas had taken on that Scottish campaign eighteen years before, had grown into a brave but reckless young man. After fighting furiously with the Dauphin's bodyguards he charged alone far beyond the English ranks to be severely wounded, captured and held to ransom by an impecunious French squire whose fortune was thus made in a lucky moment.

Released on parole after he had made a partial recovery, Maurice returned to Berkeley to raise the £1080 needed to buy his freedom—almost a year's income from the family estates. He went back to France as an unwilling guest for four more years before all was paid; a knight could not bring dishonour upon himself by breaking his parole. Maurice never fully recovered from his crippling wounds, dying eight years later.

Now sixty-five years old, Thomas Berkeley saw no more active service after Poitiers. Although Maurice's ransom payment was a setback, constant employment by the king had brought him much wealth. Payments for the services of Berkeley retainers, ransoms and plunder from French towns, wardships and profitable offices—of all these Thomas had received his more than fair share. One notable honour escaped him. He was never a member of the Most Noble Order of the Garter, founded by Edward III for twenty-six of the most gallant and honourable of his soldiers. Willing though the king was, in the interests of a united baronage, to let bygones be bygones, however atrocious, he seems to have drawn a line here.

In his castle of Berkeley Thomas lived in considerable state. His household numbered some three hundred persons: a dozen knights, each with two servants and a page, twenty-five esquires, each with one servant and a page, at least a score of men-at-arms, clerks of the chapel, officers of the household, valets and grooms. All were provided with clothing suitable to their estate: cloth of scarlet furred with the best miniver or striped red cloth trimmed with coarser miniver, coney or lamb.

To support this household a vast supply of food flowed from his thirty-five manors in Gloucestershire. Oxen, sheep, calves and lambs were killed weekly for his larders; geese, ducks, capons and peacocks came by the hundred. The fallow deer in his three parks provided the venison and his master-goatherd sent three hundred kids a year from Michaelwood. Wheat, barley and oats were needed not only for his retainers but for the hundred and more horses in the castle stables.

From the ap Adam family Thomas bought the castle and manor of Beverstone. In later life this became a favourite residence; perhaps as the years went by Berkeley with its memories of the murdered king became oppressive. He rebuilt the small Norman castle from which he could look out over the Cotswold uplands, grazed by thousands of his sheep.

John Smyth tells us that when Thomas retired from active military service he devoted himself to preparation for 'that great sleep of the grave which so good a lord could not (aided by God's mercy in Christ) but awake to immortality'. Thomas himself seems to have entertained some doubt about the sort of welcome that he was likely to receive in the next world. We have seen that after his arraignment before Parliament in 1331 he took out a form of insurance by endowing the chantry at Wortley, and in the years that followed he greatly increased the premium. The year of his acquittal was thankfully marked by many gifts to churches and chantries and to the abbey of St. Augustine at Bristol where a priest was paid to say masses for his wife Margaret and himself.

Other endowments followed; after Crecy and Calais hardly a year passed without the foundation of a chantry. When he died in 1361 at the age of sixty-eight, masses and orisons were ascending to heaven from the cathedral at Worcester, the abbey of St. Augustine, from a platoon of chaplains in the parish church just beyond the castle wall at Berkeley, from a dozen tiny places of worship in Gloucestershire, even from a lonely oratory on the Severn bank at Sheperdine where in the long winter months the cries of the wild geese mingled with the chanting of the solitary priest.

But Thomas's most splendid thank offering is the east window of the Lady Chapel of St. Augustine's Abbey, now the Cathedral of the Holy Trinity, Bristol. Here in painted glass are the arms of all those families associated with Thomas in his troubles and his successes. At the top are the arms of England, as displayed by Edward III in the early years of his reign. Immediately below in a place of honour are two Berkeley shields: of Thomas, gules, chevron and ten crosses formy argent, and of his brother Maurice, with a difference. Beneath are those of de Clare for his stepmother, Despenser for his son's bride, Clyveden for his second wife, but no acknowledgement of Margaret Mortimer.

The Berkeley rebels of the Baron's Revolt are there: Basset, de Wyllington, de la Riviere and Bradestone. The proud shield of Sir Thomas de Gournay—or, a lion rampant sable, crowned of the field with a border gules—has its place, but not that of Maltravers, unless his is the shield that has faded. One looks in vain for Mortimer until one finds him, perhaps understandably in the comparative obscurity of a small south-east window of the chapel, beside the figure of a Berkeley knight who might be his grandson Maurice. In this memorial to so many rebels are four other shields, those of the earls of the new reign: Montagu, Beauchamp, Fitzalan and de Vere, whose friendship may have helped Thomas make his peace with the young king.

Possibly all these gifts to the church were a good investment, for alone of the closely knit baronial group involved in the murder of their king the house of Berkeley has survived. Though John Maltravers left a son to inherit his lands and title, before the end of the century they were taken by an heiress, on her marriage, into the Fitzalans. The present Duke of Norfolk still holds the barony of Maltravers. When the late Duke as Earl Marshal needed additional assistance at the coronation of Elizabeth II he conjured up from the past a Maltravers Herald Extraordinary. Thus the arms of Sir John, after a lapse of five centuries, appeared again on a state occasion, in attendance upon a monarch herself descended from both Edward II and Roger Mortimer.

Nor did the barony of Bradestone long endure. That too was carried by female heirs to John Nevill, Marquess Montagu, and disappeared for ever when he was attainted of treason and executed. Thomas's little manor

Thomas (III) Lord Berkeley and his second wife, effigy in Parish Church, Berkeley

house in the hamlet of Breadstone, near Berkeley, was much altered in late medieval and Tudor times, but at its heart are the walls and beams that he knew when he sheltered his fugitive friend, Maurice.

Mortimer's grandson and heir, another Roger, was brought up as a royal ward and member of the king's household, to ensure his future loyalty. He was with the Black Prince in the Crecy campaign and when Edward III knighted his son on the battlefield the Prince in turn knighted the young Roger. Before long king and Parliament took the astonishing step of annulling the judgement of 1330 that had condemned Roger Mortimer to a traitor's death. This paved the way for the restitution of the Mortimer castles and lands and for the elevation of the young knight to that controversial earldom of March.

His son, Edward Mortimer married a granddaughter of Edward III and their son had a better claim to the throne than Henry IV, the first Lancastrian king of England, but he was wise enough to keep a low profile across the sea in Ireland, where he died in battle. He was the last male heir and the Mortimer estates and title passed through marriage to Edward IV. Since Edward's daughter married Henry VII, founder of the Tudor dynasty, the genes of Roger Mortimer the regicide passed into the royal line of England and Elizabeth II and Prince Charles count him as one of their ancestors. The ambitious and ruthless Marcher lord, if he knew this would permit himself a grim smile. But his castle of Wigmore is a neglected ruin above its green valley and the noble abbey in which he and his forbears were buried has vanished almost without trace.

But the Berkeleys outlived not merely the dangerous years after the fall of Mortimer but many later mischances and mistakes that could have brought disaster. Lord Justice Crew, delivering in 1626 a famous judgement in sonorous phrases that have echoed down the centuries, asked rhetorically, 'Where is Bohun, where's Mortimer, where's Mowbray? Nay, which is more and most of all, where is Plantagenet?' His lordship seems to have been wrong about Mowbray, which is still with us, but only a dozen or so medieval baronies have survived.

The barony of Berkeley is one of these, held now by Mary, Lady Berkeley, directly descended from the first Robert Fitzharding, and there is a male heir. Ancient baronies created by writ of summons to Parliament can be inherited by the female line. And there are still Berkeleys in the castle by the Severn.

That they are today in possession of the castle and a goodly part of their medieval manors after eight hundred years is so remarkable that this story must end with a brief account of the fortunes of the family since the death of Thomas. His son did not long survive him but his grandson, Thomas IV, who held the barony for almost forty years, so handled his affairs that he became the wealthiest and most influential of all the early Berkeleys, and a military commander of great distinction. When a French fleet was sent to the aid of Owen Glendower, then in revolt against English rule, Thomas as Admiral commanding the southern coasts completely destroyed it in a battle near Milford Haven. He was interested in the sea and kept his own ship moored at the mouth of the Little Avon, sailing for pleasure on the Severn.

Thomas was truly a man for all campaigns; we find him as 'General Commander and Ingineer' in charge of operations against the castles held by Glendower's men. His last commission was to gather a force of Gloucestershire men and lead them to the great battle of Agincourt. It was at Berkeley Castle that a group of barons met to agree on the deposition of Richard II, who like his great-grandfather was hunted down and murdered, to be replaced on the throne by Henry IV.

By his marriage to Margaret, sole heiress to the barony of the Lisle, he added twenty-four manors and many farms and lands to the Berkeley domains. At the castle he led a 'stately and sumptuous life' enjoying in the family tradition hunting and all the other sports of the field. He left no son when he died in 1417 and the Berkeley manors passed by entail to his nephew James.

His daughter Elizabeth, married to Richard Beauchamp, the most powerful nobleman in England, of course inherited her father's Lisle manors and immediately laid claim to much more, thus inaugurating what John Smyth described as 'bluddy brawls and lawsuits of one hundred and ninety-two years agitation'. While the Wars of the Roses raged and governments lost control of much of the country, the Berkeleys and the Lisle claimants fought their own private wars in law courts, in skirmishes and in plundering raids, culminating in 1470 in the Battle of Nibley Green, near Wotton-under-Edge, the last 'private' feudal battle to be fought on English soil.

The young Viscount Lisle and more than a hundred of his men were killed, leaving William, Lord Berkeley in possession of all the disputed lands. Though Lisle left no direct heir his claim was maintained by his widow and her relatives; William had to keep them quiet by paying annuities. Later, rather than join Henry Tudor in rebellion, William chose to remain loyal to his king, Richard III, and was present with him on the battlefield of Bosworth when Richard was killed.

Henry VII was not the man to forget this. This combined pressures of royal disfavour and the continuing Lisle claims led William to make a will leaving almost all the Berkeley lands to Henry and his male heirs. For sixty years they were in the possession of the Crown and might have remained so to this day had not the boy king Edward VI died unmarried, when they returned to the Berkeleys.

Even so, after a few years Queen Elizabeth successfully reclaimed certain manors and conferred them on her favourite, the Earl of Leicester and his brother, who had inherited the Lisle claim. This brought about another forty years of conflict about doubtful boundaries, fighting between retainers of each side and complicated lawsuits involving, according to John Smyth, much forgery, perjury and corruption of judges and juries. At last both parties tired of the conflict and Henry, Lord Berkeley bought out the Lisle claim for a cash payment. Each side had spent more money than the manors were worth.

Though the castle was held for a time by the Royalists the Berkeley estates escaped confiscation during the Civil Wars; the Lord Berkeley of the time was living abroad and took no part in the struggle. The only penalty imposed was the demilitarisation of the castle by cutting the great breach in the outer wall of the keep.

His successor was rewarded with an earldom for his part in bringing Charles II back to England, but the Berkeleys abandoned James II when William of Orange came to England. Throughout the eighteenth century they were members of the governing Whig aristocracy. It was then that the fourth earl inherited the London property of the Cornish branch of the family, twenty acres that included much of Berkeley Square and nearby Mayfair streets. All this, added to the farms of the Severn Vale, soon doubled the family income.

Everything seemed to point to a future for the Berkeleys as one of the wealthy, politically influential Whig families but in 1796 the fifth earl, Frederick Augustus, married a young woman named Mary Cole who had for some years been his mistress and had borne him several children, a liaison that led to more than a hundred years of tangled and much-publicised family history. Attempts made in 1796 and 1811 to persuade the

House of Lords to accept an alleged earlier marriage that would have made Mary's first son, William Fitzhardinge, heir to the earldom both failed, as did three later petitions, the last in 1891. By the will of Frederick Augustus the castle and the Gloucestershire estates were inherited by William and remained in the possession of the Fitzhardinges, as the children born before the accepted marriage were called, until 1917 when the line died out.

Before this the earldom and the Mayfair estate had passed to Randal Mowbray Berkeley, a young naval officer descended from a brother of Frederick Augustus. The eight earl used his new wealth to build his own laboratory at Oxford, embarking on scientific research that brought him a Fellowship of the Royal Society. When in 1917 he inherited the castle and its lands he began yet another career as territorial magnate, Master of the Berkeley Hunt and amateur architect.

Randal spent vast sums of money on a thoroughgoing restoration of Berkeley Castle and a very necessary modernisation of the domestic living arrangements. To pay for all this and other expensive projects he sold his Mayfair acres for a reputed £2,000,000, and more than eight thousant acres of his Gloucestershire inheritance for another £280,000. Had all this been retained, its proper management would have made the Berkeleys one of the richest families of the old nobility.

The eighth earl on his death in 1942 left the castle and the remaining estate to Captain Robert Berkeley, head of the Worcestershire branch of the family founded in the fifteenth century by a young brother of William, the victor of Nibley Green. He was succeeded by his son, Mr. John Berkeley, the present incumbent who is twenty-fourth in the direct male line of descent from that Robert Fitzharding for whom Henry II built the castle beside the Severn.

Thirty years ago the historian H.P.R. Finberg wrote: 'When the proposed atomic power station is built within sight of (Berkeley's) windows, the past and the future will confront each other more dramatically perhaps than anywhere in England.' The power station was built, has run its useful life and is now to be demolished. It may be a hundred years before grass grows again over its site but the castle that Shakespeare saw 'by yon tuft of trees' will still be there and it will be no matter for surprise if a Berkeley is still at the window, looking out on his ancestral lands.

SOURCES

FOURTEENTH CENTURY CHRONICLES

Chronicles of the reigns of Edward I and Edward II
Ed. W. Stubbs. Rolls Series 1882.
>> Gesta Edwardi di Carnarvan
>> Annales Paulini
>> Annales Londinienses
Vita Edwardi Secundi, ed. N. D. Young. 1957
Chronicon: Geoffrey le Baker, ed. EM. Thompson, 1889.
Continuatio Chronicarum: A. Murimuth, ed. E. M. Thompson, 1889.
Chronicles: Jean Froissart.
Polychronicon: Ranulph Higden. Rolls Series, 1865–86.

LATER WORKS

A. Benedetti: Eduardo d'Inghilterra. 1921.
Davies, J. C.: The Baronial Opposition to Edward II. 1918.
McKisack, M.: The Fourteenth Century (Oxford History), 1959.
Rees, W.: South Wales and the March, 1284–1415. 1924.
Smyth, J.: Lives of the Berkeleys, ed. Maclean. 1893.
Tout, T. F.: Captivity and Death of Edward of Caernarvon,
>> Collected Papers, 1920.
Wright, T.: Rolls of Arms. . . Siege of Caerlaverock. 1864.

MISCELLANEOUS

Archaelogia, Vol. L. S. A. Moore: Documents relating to the death and burial of
>> Edward II.
English Historical Review.
>> Vol. XXI.   F. J. Tanqueray: Conspiracy of Thomas Dunhead.
>> Vol. XXVI.   Arrest of Roger Mortimer.
Modern Language Review.
>> Vol. XXXIV.   An Anglo-Norman Poem by Edward II.
Trans. Bristol & Glos. Archaeological Society.
>> Vol. XLVIII.   St. Clair Baddeley: Berkeley Castle.
Trans. Royal Historical Society.
>> Vol. IX, 3rd Series. J. C. Davies: The Despenser War in Glamorgan.

INDEX